Garden Angel

Grow Your Passion for Gardening

*"The love of gardening is
a seed once sown that never dies."*

Gertrude Jekyll

*"When the world wearies and society
fails to satisfy, there is always the
garden."*

Minnie Aumonier

CAROLE BARR

First published in Great Britain in 2024

Editing, Design, typesetting and publishing by UK Book Publishing.

www.ukbookpublishing.com

ISBN: 978-1-917329-10-1

To Mel.

Garden with love
Carde x

For Esme and Seamus
Here we are, huddled together
wherever we go

Contents

Introduction

"Odd as I am sure it will appear to some, I can think of no better form of personal involvement in the cure of the environment than that of gardening. A person who is growing a garden, if he is growing it organically, is improving a piece of the world."

Wendell Berry

"Everything that slows us down and forces patience, everything that sets us back into the slow circles of nature, is a help. Gardening is an instrument of grace."

May Sarton

I love gardening. If I ever feel down or need to find some space or peace, I head into the garden. I always feel more relaxed, happy and at peace when I have been outside in the garden, whether I am carrying out tasks or just strolling around it. If there is anything I should do more of in the garden, then it is to sit still, have a cup of tea and just take it all in. The term forest bathing describes going into a forest or wood and immersing yourself in the sights, sounds and aroma of the forest, which in turn brings a sense of well-being and balance. Being in nature causes our bodies to release positive hormones which improves our overall mental wellbeing and in turn increases our physical health. I believe the same is true when we spend time in our garden spaces and tending to our plants. It doesn't matter what size of garden you have access to, by tending it and providing a habitat for wildlife, you will increase your dopamine levels and overall sense of well-being.

Let me introduce myself, I am Carole, The Garden Angel and I have been gardening professionally for more than 20 years. I would like to bring some of the knowledge and techniques that I have developed over that time to you. I wasn't always an enthusiastic gardener; I did see looking after my small city garden as a bit of a chore. In fact, and I shudder to remember this, I used to get my parents to come and cut my grass for me! The fact was, I didn't know what I was doing, I didn't have a vision for the garden, and the whole experience of gardening was very flat and not fulfilling at all. I saw gardening as a chore.

At that time I worked in a corporate environment and we were encouraged to carry out volunteer work, so I chose to volunteer as a gardener for the RNIB. I now can't remember why this is the area I chose, but it must have been fate! I was given a garden to look after for a lovely couple, Ann and Alex. They were both keen gardeners and were able to keep me right, help name plants and instil some of their love of gardening in me. I then started to enjoy my garden and look at ways to make it look better. My job at the time involved researching, so it came naturally to me to start 'learning' about gardening. This was before the internet became a part of daily life, so this meant borrowing books from the library and, of course, watching Gardeners' World. I was hooked. So, when I left my job I decided to start up my own gardening business, maintaining gardens and designing new planting schemes here we are more than 20 years later.

As well as learning to love gardening, discovering new plant varieties and creating beautiful spaces for people, I think the key aspect of gardening to me (both professionally and personally) is the great sense of peace that it brings. I feel in tune with the rhythm of nature when I am gardening. To see the seasons turn, plants emerge from the soil, flowering then set seed, to put the 'garden to bed' for the winter, all seems so natural that I can forget everything else that may cause me stress. Growing my own fruit and vegetables has caused me to look at how we are treating our soil, that food waste is a crime and to appreciate everything that goes into producing food as a whole. Fruit and vegetables grown in your own garden do taste sweeter than some of those produced en masse. The sense of achievement when you pick your first ripe tomato or eat a ripe strawberry still warm from the sun is enormous. I am smiling, just thinking about this.

Are you someone who sees gardening as a chore? Something that just has to be done? A task to be ticked off the to-do list? Or are you someone who would like to enjoy your garden space but are a little daunted or overwhelmed with the right and wrong way to garden? Where to even start? What the heck do these strange gardening terms mean? These are all comments and thoughts that people have shared with me over the years, and I really would love for everyone interested in starting to garden alongside nature, or increasing their gardening skills and knowledge, to have the confidence to jump right in and have a go.

My aim with this book is to take the fear out of gardening, to show that it is possible to create a beautiful space for you to immerse yourself in and to show you how to give back to nature. Use this book as your guide to discover your passion for gardening. Take it with you outside and into your garden space, get the pages grubby, write your own notes in it and keep a note of your progress. Each of us, no matter the size of our garden space, can make a positive impact on the climate, nature and our own wellbeing.

For this book, I have only referred to myself carrying out tasks in my garden, but I would like to thank Seamus (my husband) for all of his hard work and input –without which we wouldn't have any paths or patios or raised beds or a polytunnel. It is our garden, our sanctuary, and we both get so much pleasure and peace from being in it. Thank you, S.

Chapter One

Getting Comfortable with Gardening Terms

"Take chances, make mistakes. That's how you grow."

Mary Tyler Moore

"There are no gardening mistakes, only experiments."

Janet Kilburn Phillips

I often hear people saying that 'there are so many rules to gardening, how do I know if I am doing the right thing?'. Well, there are different ways to grow different kinds of plants and there are certain times of the year to carry out jobs. But this shouldn't put you off having a go. We learn by trying new things and yes, sometimes making mistakes. This book is all about giving you the tools and information to take those first steps towards creating a space that will give you more back than you can imagine. If you understand the basics, then over time you will learn more gardening skills. If you are just starting out, then try growing one type of plant and once you feel more confident add in another type and so on.

It is also really useful to ask other people for their hints and tips and what their gardening hacks are. How do they deal with a particular issue? I have learnt so much from listening to others talk about their gardens and gardening. Not only professional gardeners, but customers, friends and family. Everyone has their little nugget of information. Swapping ideas and plants is a very satisfying thing to do. But, sometimes you will hear people pronouncing things like, 'Of course this plant needs ericaceous conditions', or 'I like to mulch in the spring', and you can think, good grief I only understood about 50% of that. Don't be shy, ask. Or more importantly, read this book!

Let's look at some of the gardening terms you may have heard about and wondered what they meant.

▧ Evergreen

Evergreen plants are those that keep their leaves all year round. Though technically they don't! They will drop their older leaves during the year, but they will have new leaves on the plant, so they will remain evergreen to our eyes. Currently my Photinia Red Robin is shedding a lot of leaves! But the new growth is on this large shrub, so it still has a full head of hair so to speak. If there is a prolonged dry spell, then they may shed leaves to accommodate the, hopefully, short-term water supply issues. Evergreen shrubs provide structure to the garden throughout the year and are a really important part of any planting scheme. Some evergreen shrubs flower, others don't.

■ Deciduous

Deciduous plants drop their leaves in autumn and then they become dormant. They will produce new leaf growth in the spring of the following year. These plants are equally important in a garden planting scheme, as some have beautiful structures in the form of their stems which will provide winter interest. For example, the humble Cornus has beautiful red, orange or green/yellow stems in winter. I love Acers when they drop their leaves as you can marvel at the twisting stems which are exposed during the winter months. These shapes tell the story of the plant or tree, where they have been pruned or changed the direction of growth to get more sunlight or avoid a too close neighbour.

▨ Shrubs

Shrubs are small to medium-sized woody plants. When I say woody plants, this means that the stems will appear in varying shades of brown and will not be flexible. Unlike the stems of perennials (see below) which will be green, soft and flexible. They grow from the ground with multiple stems. Hydrangeas and Philadelphus are examples of deciduous shrubs, and Pittisporum and Rhodendron are evergreen shrubs. There will be buds along the stems from which leaves and flowers will grow. They can be evergreen or deciduous. They can produce flowers or just have leaf interest. They can be pruned to keep them in shape and to the size you want them to be. More on pruning in Chapter 7. Deciduous shrubs are also an important feature in the winter garden and will complement your evergreen structure.

▨ Trees

Like shrubs, trees are woody plants, but they are grown as single-stem specimens. They are much larger than shrubs and you can get evergreen and deciduous varieties. Some trees produce blossoms or flowers and fruit. Trees can also be pruned to keep their shape and maintain their size. When choosing a tree, it is important to look at the height and spread as it matures, as you do not want to have something unsuitable for the size of your garden. Trees are especially good in gardens as they provide height and a focal point, as well as shade during the hotter months. There is something magical about the sounds of the gentle rustle of tree leaves on a warm summer day. It gives you such an uplift. Even if your garden is small, do not discount having a tree somewhere in the garden as there are so many varieties there will be one that suits your particular garden. There are many small to medium varieties of flowering Cherry trees and crab apple trees. These provide height, blossom and in the case of the Malus you will get small fruit. Planting a large tree or shrub in a smaller garden has the effect of making the garden seem larger as it plays with the perspective of the garden. The brain thinks this garden must be big as there is a tree growing in it.

▓ Flowering perennials

A perennial is a plant which will survive more than two years; shrubs and trees come into this category as they live for two years and more, but here we are describing the flowering perennial where the soft new growth comes from the base of the plant and unlike the shrub, it is not woody. Hardy Geraniums and Geums are long flowering perennials which are easy to grow. As perennials grow from the base each year, they put their energy into growing flower heads and this is where you will get your yearly show of colour. Once established, they can be lifted out of the ground and divided to provide more plants. More on this in Chapter 6.

▓ Biennials

A biennial is a plant which produces its leaves in the first year and it completes its life cycle in the second year when it produces its flowers. If you let the flowers produce seeds, then these will fall to the ground and the cycle begins again. I was given some Honesty seeds one year as well as a couple of seedlings. The seedlings produced flowers in the next year, the seeds produced seedlings in that same year. Then the seed heads of that year's flowers were left to fall. And now I have Honesty flowering every year whilst the new seedlings grow away in other parts of the garden.

▓ Annuals

These plants grow, produce flowers and die in one year. You can save the seeds of annuals to sow the following year – more details in Chapter 5. Some examples of annuals are Calendula, Cosmos and Poppies. All provide long-lasting colour to the garden. Using annuals in your garden will give you a sumptuous burst of colour throughout the summer months and into autumn. They can fill gaps whilst your borders are maturing or provide colour where spring flowering plants have finished flowering. Once autumn comes, you can dig them up and compost them.

Bulbs

Bulbs are planted under the ground and contain all the necessary food and genetic information to form a stem which will break through the surface of the soil. It will continue to grow and produce a flower, then once the flower has gone over the leaves will die back and the bulb will remain dormant until the next year. It is important to deadhead the bulb as you want the energy from the leaves and stem to go back into the bulb for next year's display. If you are looking to naturalise, say, Narcissus in a lawn, then don't deadhead and the seeds will fall and hopefully grow into a bulb to increase your stock.

Mulch

A mulch is a general term for covering the soil with a natural substance, normally compost or soil conditioner. When someone says to put a good layer of mulch, this would be a depth of two inches. I mulch to help improve the soil structure and health. Mulching will also help to retain moisture around the plants as well as keeping weeds in check. Mulch can also be wood bark which is decorative but has no benefits in terms of improving the condition of the soil. It can even be a layer of cardboard placed over the ground to prevent weeds from growing. Not the most stylish of looks, but is very useful if you have an area of ground with invasive weeds such as ground elder. As no light is allowed through, this will weaken the weed and if you keep the area covered for a couple of years you will see much less or even no more ground elder. You can add a thick layer of cardboard down and then cover this with a good thick layer of bark mulch, which is more pleasing to the eye. Mulching your garden is one of the best things you can do for it. I mulch in the autumn and then again in the spring and pretty much don't have to weed throughout the growing season.

▨ Deadheading

This is the act of cutting the spent flower heads from a shrub, rose or perennial. Make a clean cut and always cut back to something, the next bud or leaf joint. The main reason for deadheading is to stop the formation of a seed head. Unless of course, you want a seed head! Why would you want a seed head? You may be collecting seed or wish to leave the seed head for the birds to enjoy. See Chapter 5 on growing plants from seed. Deadheading spent flowers will encourage more flowers to form as the plant wants to produce seeds. I deadhead throughout the summer months, as I go into autumn I will leave the flower heads to form seeds which will help the birds over winter.

Pruning

Deadheading is a form of pruning, for the reasons I mentioned in the paragraph above. Pruning of shrubs is carried out to improve their shape or form as is the case with trees. You will also prune to take out any crossing stems – those that are diseased, dying, or dead. Pruning also encourages fresh growth and flower production. It is also extremely important for airflow within a plant or tree. More on this in Chapter 7.

Lifting and dividing

This refers to perennials and bulbs. Where they have outgrown their position, when you want to increase your stock or when they need a refresh as they have slowed or stopped flowering. Taking a fork or a spade, carefully lift the plant out of the ground, avoiding too much damage to the roots. Then with a spade or two forks back-to-back, divide the plant up into smaller plants. You can then replant a small section in the original position and distribute it around the garden, or give it away to friends. Chapter 7 will go into more detail on lifting and dividing to increase your stock.

Crown lifting

Simply put, this is the removal of the lower branches of a tree or shrub. You are effectively raising the crown or area of leaf growth further from the ground. This is done to improve the shape, to allow more light to the area under the tree or shrub, can allow for new planting under the plant or to allow access under a tree for grass cutting for example. I am a big fan of crown lifting. I often lift the crown of my multi-stem shrubs to gain light and air underneath them or to expose the structure of the stems. As a tree matures, you can remove some lower branches to make walking past them easier.

Staking and plant supports

Some perennials will need to be supported as the weight of their flower heads can cause them to flop down. And you want to see the flowers! It also stops them from lying on top of other plants which could harm them. Plant supports should be in place before too much new growth is produced. This will prevent you from breaking any new growth by staking later in the year. I put in plant supports in March and April at the latest. The plants will simply grow up through or within the supports if done early in spring. Plant supports come in various shapes and sizes. I find the round grow-through support useful when used for supporting Sedum, Lupins, Peony roses and Delphiniums. The other type is a half-circle support – these can be interconnected to produce a circle, but I tend to just use the half-circle for my Knautia, Aquilegia, Hellebore and Leucanthemums. They are also useful to keep perennials from falling over your lawn.

Newly planted trees should always be staked. The reason for this is to avoid wind rock. When inserting your tree stake, make sure that you don't have it go through the roots, place it to the side of the root ball and hammer in securely. Use a tree strap or tie to secure the tree to the stake, and always have a divider between the tree and stake to stop the tree rubbing on the stake.

▨ Grass cutting

In spring and autumn you should not cut the grass short – keep the blades high and cut only to even out the growth. This is purely for aesthetic purposes as grass very rarely grows at an even rate. The choice of whether to use an electric, petrol or battery-powered mower is a personal one and will depend on the size of the lawn you are cutting. The key thing is to make sure that the blades are sharp or you will tear the grass. You should avoid cutting the grass when it is raining or the ground is very wet. Cutting grass too short can encourage the accumulation of moss and encourage lawn weeds. It is recommended that the ideal height that grass is cut to is 1-1.5 inches, slightly longer if there is a lot of traffic on the lawn. In chapter 3 I will talk more about lawns and working alongside nature.

Aeration

This is done to avoid compaction in lawns and can be done with a machine which will take out small cores or with a fork pushed into the ground and move around to create a small hole in the lawn. This should be followed up by brushing in some lawn sand. This will stop water pooling in the newly made holes and allow the roots to recover.

Scarifying

This is the act of raking out the dead growth or thatch. It also removes moss. Again, you can use a machine or use a metal tine rake. I scarify the lawn in the autumn – this allows the lawn to recover over the winter months. If you scarify in the spring, and the spring is very dry, you can put undue stress on the lawn and it can inhibit new growth.

Crop Rotation

You will have come across this term if you have ever grown your own vegetables. Although the first time I remember hearing the term was in a Geography class at high school! It only became relevant when I started growing vegetables in my own garden. Simply put, it is the rotation of different types of crops across each new growing season. Crops have differing nutrient needs and it also prevents disease and/or bug attacks. I will go into this in more detail in Chapter 9.

Companion planting

This term is widely used when growing vegetables and fruit. It is when you plant crops of different types alongside each other to deter insect/slug damage and also help prevent diseases affecting your crops. It has the added benefit that it will help with pollination and, in turn, maximise your harvest. You can also use flowering plants in companion planting. More details on this in Chapter 9.

Photosynthesis

Plants need exposure to sunlight, carbon dioxide from the atmosphere and water to form carbohydrates (sugars) for growth, flower or fruit production and then to release oxygen into the atmosphere. If we are growing any plants either from seed or container, to ensure its healthy growth it must have all of these factors available to it. You will notice that deciduous plants – those that drop their leaves at the end of the year – and perennials only start to grow once the levels of sunlight increase at the start of spring. And, equally, they will drop their leaves and die back as the light levels decrease in the autumn. If you are growing anything from seed, you must provide sunlight, carbon dioxide and water so that the seed can germinate, and produce stem growth and leaves.

▦ My top tools for the garden

The list below is what I find to be the most useful and necessary tools for gardening. The list could be longer, but as a starting point for you, I thought this would be useful. It is important to find the right tool for the jobs you will be carrying out. Find the right size and weight which suits you; this is important.

Buying new tools can be expensive so I would suggest only getting the tools that are necessary to get you started. You can build up your stock of tools over time. Keep an eye out for people selling or giving away second-hand tools.

1. **Border fork and border spade**. These are smaller than your ordinary fork and spade. They can get into smaller spaces and I find them lighter to use.

2. **A pointed spade** is a new purchase of mine. This is a spade with a point rather than a flat edge. It makes breaking hard ground much

easier and will cut through any small roots you may come across. A really great tool for planting new shrubs and trees. The shaft has a slight bend in it, which gives it more leverage if you come across some very heavy soil and is kinder to your back.

3. **Secateurs**. Whatever you choose, you must keep your secateurs sharp and clean. I have had my secateurs for 15 years now and they are still going strong. When you are choosing secateurs, it is important to have the right size for your hands. I use Felco Classic 8 secateurs. These fit my hands perfectly, they are weighted well and are bypass blades. Like any of the tools I am mentioning, I have my preferred make and model. But you must find what suits you best. To avoid losing my secateurs, I have a pouch for them which clips onto my belt. This makes sure that I know exactly where they are and haven't thrown them in the garden waste bin by mistake, which has happened on more occasions than I like to admit! Nobody wants to find themselves rummaging through their garden waste bin.

4. **Loppers**. These come in various shapes and sizes. I prefer to use bypass loppers as

they give me the cleanest cut on live wood. I use a set that is light in weight – if you are doing a lot of cutting you will notice if your loppers are too heavy. Anvil loppers are better for cutting dead wood. You can also get extendable loppers, for reaching stems higher up, but I have found these to be quite heavy. I also have a long-reach cutter. This is extendable to around five metres and you use the long rope attachment to enable the cutting action. I use this on tree pruning where I do not want or cannot use a ladder.

5. **Hori hori**. This is great for planting bulbs, for removing perennial weeds from borders and lawns; it has a serrated edge for doing light cutting as well. I also use a tool called a Kirpi, which is very difficult to source, but if you can get one, you will not be disappointed.

6. **Long-handled hand fork and trowel**. I prefer the long-handled versions of the ubiquitous fork and trowel. You get more traction when working and it saves bending down as much.

7. **Hoe**. If you wish to hoe off weeds from the surface of the soil, then a Dutch hoe is the most popular type of hoe. I tend to just hand

weed, but if I want to hoe the weeds off of the surface I use a swoe, which I find much easier on my back. It has three sharp edges and you use it in a push-pull action. It is great for getting in between plants. Always make sure your hoe or swoe has the right length of shaft for your height: this will stop you from hunching over. It is also important to keep the edges of your hoe/swoe sharp.

8. **Hand shears**. These also come in many shapes and sizes. I again go for a light pair and keep them very sharp and oiled. These are used for shaping shrubs, light hedge-cutting duties or a bit of topiary.

9. **A mattock** is not an essential tool to have, but it is an extremely useful one to have around if you are digging very heavy soil. This was the tool I had to use in our garden when I first started to plant it. The clay soil was so heavy and compacted, that the only way for me to dig a hole for planting was to use my mattock to break up the soil. I also used it when I was levelling some of the areas for putting down slabs. It is also excellent for digging out large roots. I am very fond of my mattock; it has helped me out on so many occasions.

10. **A hand saw or woodcutter** is also very useful to have in your tool armoury. Any stems that are just too big for your loppers will be cut very easily with a hand saw. There are again, many different varieties to choose from. The blades are normally easy enough to replace if they lose sharpness. Although you can sharpen them yourself. Most, if not all, have the cutting action on the pull towards you.

11. **Rakes** come in various shapes and sizes. There is the metal tine rake which is very good for raking out moss and thatch from lawns. There is the garden rake, which has shorter teeth and is very good for raking over the soil to remove stones or level the area out, such as a vegetable bed in preparation for sowing seeds. There are also leaf rakes which are excellent for raking leaves from lawns and the border. The teeth of these rakes are made of plastic and help prevent damage to plants. I use all three types of rakes for the different jobs around the garden.

12. **A good brush** is essential, I think, for around the garden. Keep your pathways and patios clear of debris. It's a much more satisfying

and wildlife-friendly way to remove debris than using a blower.

13. **With safety in mind,** I would like to recommend that you invest in some gloves. I have avoided some nasty injuries by wearing gloves to work in the garden. I know a lot of people prefer to garden without gloves and that is ok, but if you garden frequently then you do increase your chances of cuts and abrasions. I have gloves for summer, winter, wet weather and pruning anything with thorns! If I am using a hedge cutter or cutting large branches, I wear a pair of safety glasses. Again, through experience, I have had a couple of injuries to my eyes so I am more cautious now. If you are using a petrol hedge cutter or mower, then think about wearing some ear defenders. Finally, if you are kneeling to carry out garden work, then knee pads are a must – damp knees will come back to haunt you one day! A kneeling pad is an alternative, but the pads mean you don't have to keep moving the kneeling pad around.

14. **Wheelbarrows and trugs** will help you collect and move materials around the

garden. Don't be tempted to carry very heavy loads around the garden – if you do have to move, say, bags of compost or heavy plants, then a wheelbarrow will make this task much easier. I always have two trugs or buckets with me when I am working in the garden. One is to collect materials that can go in the compost heap, and the other is for the weeds and seed heads which don't go on the compost heap.

15. **Your body** is your most valuable tool and you should be aware of your limitations and when to take a break or stretch. Be aware of how you are moving around the garden, and try not to twist your body or to over-stretch. Only lift what you feel comfortable with; if it's too heavy or awkward, then get some help or deploy your wheelbarrow. Stretching regularly sounds obvious, but it's very easy to get so immersed in what you are doing that you can forget to stand up straight and stretch, as you would when doing any form of exercise. Gardening is very good for you both mentally and physically, but remember to take a break, stretch, enjoy the view and take time to enjoy everything around you.

Cleaning and sharpening hand tools

Once you have your tools, remember to look after them, they are a big investment. I always clean them after I have used them by wiping them down with a cloth or towel to remove sap or soil, and then I apply a little bit of oil. It is also important to keep your hand tools sharp. I have explained below how I maintain my hand tools.

Abrasive stone

I use an abrasive stone to remove sap and any rust from my hand tools. This looks like a big eraser you'd get in a stationery set. It comes in different grades; I use a fine grade but a coarser grade will remove tougher areas of rust. You can also use a wire brush – this is useful to use on spades. Wire wool is also ideal for this job. Rub the area with the stone until all the sap and/or rust has been removed.

Sharpening stone

I use a diamond-cut sharpening stone which comes with a handle; I find this easier to use. You can buy sharpening stones without handles or they come as a sharpening block. The sharpening stone I use can be used dry and has a coarse side and a smoother finishing side. The sharpening blocks tend to need to be kept wet to be effective. Choose whichever you feel would suit you and your budget. I use the coarse side first, sweeping the stone along the edge of the blade away from me, then repeat on the other side of the blade. I then use the smoother side, sweeping away from me to create a smooth, sharp finish.

▨ Oil the surface

Finally, you should add a thin layer of oil to the surface of the sharpened tool. I use camellia oil as this doesn't run off the surface and won't leave a sticky residue. This is useful as I have used spray oils before and if they run onto the handles of the tools it makes them difficult to use. The oil will form a barrier to repel sap and water, and therefore rust is less likely to set in.

Cleaning and sharpening tools using an abrasive stone,
sharpening stone and camellia oil

▦ Top 7 Key Points from Chapter One

1. Don't be put off by new terms or perceived 'rules' of gardening. Ask for help and advice, watch gardening programmes, or read gardening books.

2. The terms evergreen and deciduous refer to trees, shrubs and perennials. Evergreen plants keep their leaves year-round and deciduous plants will drop their leaves and become dormant in the winter.

3. Biennials will grow their leaves in their first year and in year two they will flower, drop their seeds and die.

4. Annuals will grow, flower, set seed and die in the same year.

5. Bulbs store their energy and genetic material underground within the fleshy bulb. Deadhead to ensure the energy from the dying leaves returns to the bulb, which will encourage strong growth and flowering next year.

6. Think carefully about the garden tools you need to get started, buy the best you can

afford and look after them by cleaning them and keeping the edges sharp.

7. Gardening is something to enjoy, so don't give yourself too much work to do or worry that you don't know enough. Start with one job, one plant, one hand tool. Your gardening knowledge will grow alongside your garden space.

This chapter aims to start you on your journey to engage with gardening and to feel comfortable around some of the terms used by other gardeners. Gardening is meant to be a positive and enjoyable experience and I aim to give you the confidence to make that first start, whatever size your garden space is. Some jobs can seem overwhelming, but there are methods and techniques which we will cover in the rest of the book, should make them much easier to carry out.

Notes

_____

_____

_____

_____

_____

_____

_____

_____

_____

_____

_____

_____

_____

_____

_____

_____

_____

Chapter Two

Soil Health

"To forget how to dig the earth and to tend the soil is to forget ourselves."

Mahatma Gandhi

"The soil is the great connector of lives, the source and destination of all."

Wendell Berry

It is quite shocking how much we have depleted the nutrients and the structure in soil and we can see the effects that this is having across the world, not only on food production but also the depletion of pollinators, flooding and drought conditions. The use of chemicals, not only by companies but by individuals in their garden has equally had an impact. But soil is our foundation for having a healthy garden, whether it is for plants or growing our food. If we get the soil health right, then everything else will follow. I am not here to discuss the global soil health situation, but I really would like to give you a few pointers to help improve the soil in your garden. What do I mean by soil health? Surely by its very nature soil is healthy? Generally, yes it is. However, if the soil has been cultivated in the past then there may be deficits in nutrients and soil structure. Compaction from heavy footfall over the years of an area that has been turned into a border. Double digging was once extremely popular amongst gardeners, but this can lead to the disruption of the soil layers. It may be that your garden was once farmland (greenfield site) or industrial land (brownfield site), all these factors will contribute to the health of the soil in your garden. If you have had to make changes to the topography of your garden and moved areas of soil around to create a more level surface or terracing on larger slopes, the soil might not be at its healthiest.

All of these things can harm the health of your soil. By getting to know the structure of your soil, you will have a better understanding of your soil health and what steps to take to improve it.

Soil is made up of different layers, each with its characteristics and functions. For this book, I have divided the layers into three levels. There are many reference books which will go into much more detail. But I feel that for our purposes and about domestic gardening I will describe the three layers that are of most interest to us.

▧ Layer one

The top layer of soil is referred to as topsoil which is made up of humus. This contains organic matter including decomposed leaves, perennial dieback, small twigs, old flower heads etc. If you add your own or nursery-bought compost to mulch the borders, then this adds to the humus layer which in turn increases the biological activity and therefore the structure and health of the soil. What do you mean, biological activity?! I am talking about bacteria, insects, and worms. These guys are responsible for consuming and breaking down the natural debris that falls on the surface of the soil. In healthy soil, this layer of topsoil will be high in mineral content due to the organic material and bacterial, insect and worm activity. It is normally dark in appearance and has a crumbling texture.

▧ Layer two

This is referred to as subsoil and as you would imagine lies just below the topsoil. This is where you will find the small particles of clay, silt and sand. This layer will contain much less organic material, but you will find finer minerals such as carbonates, iron and gypsum. There will be small stones in this layer which can help with drainage. Your soil type is determined by the percentages of clay, silt and sand. I will go into more detail on this later in this chapter. If the soil has been dug or turned over, then you may find that these two layers become mixed. This is not too big an issue if you stop digging and turning over and just keep adding to the top layer. All will balance itself out in the long run. The plant roots will go as far as the subsoil.

Layer three

This next layer is often referred to as the parent material. This is where you will find the small stones and rocks which have risen up when they break down from the bedrock. The roots of plants will not go down into this layer as there are no nutrients and it is compacted.

By understanding the soil structure you can start to see that deep digging and turning the soil over can have huge effects on its overall health and ultimately how well your plants will thrive. It is also really important to keep the structure loose, avoiding compaction as this will lead to the leaching of nutrients when the rain will wash them away. Compaction of your soil will also lead to a lack of oxygen and affect the microorganisms within the soil. So, when I talk about making sure the soil is healthy and the structure is good, then this is where I am coming from. And because the roots of our plants and trees will only go into the first two layers, we must make sure that these layers are as deep as they can be.

◼ What type of soil do you have?

Now that you have an understanding of the different layers in your soil, it is important to find out what type of soil you have. What do I mean by this and why is it important, I hear you ask.

As we have seen your soil is made up of sand, clay, and silt, and depending on the proportions of each in your soil will determine the texture of the soil that you have. There is a very easy way to see what type of soil you have.

Take a handful of soil, and shape it into a ball in your hand. If it remains in shape then you have predominantly clay soil. If it doesn't form a ball shape, then it is sandy soil. The ideal soil is loamy. This is the holy grail, where you have good proportions of clay providing the nutrients, and sand and silt to provide the drainage. This soil retains its shape enough to form a ball, but you can easily crumble it in between your fingers.

Take samples of soil from different areas of your garden – you may find that you have slightly varying soil types in your garden.

Take my own example: I bought a new house and garden, built on a former farmer's field. But there had been little or no working of the soil carried out for years, it was mainly used to graze farm animals. There was very little topsoil – most of this had been removed during the build process or dug into the clay soil. On the plus side, I had clay soil. This is very nutrient-rich. But it does come with its problems. Drainage and compaction are two of these.

So, how did I get around this? I do not 'dig' the garden at all, I do not even hoe the garden. I have year-on-year added organic material to the surface of the soil and let nature do its job. There is bacterial activity which breaks down the organic matter, worms come up and take the organic matter down into the subsoil where the insects and microbes can get to work. I just hand-pick any weeds that appear, I use my hori hori to remove any perennial weeds and their roots.

The structure of the soil has improved, there is no hard baking of the soil (clay soil is prone to this in periods of dry weather), nor is there runoff of water when it rains and therefore no leaching of the nutrients. I have increased the depth of the topsoil by mulching and the bacterial and worm activity has loosened the structure of the subsoil. What do I use to mulch the garden? My homemade compost – more of this in Chapter 8. I don't remove any fallen leaves in the border (I only remove leaves that have fallen onto the perennial plants as this could cause rotting of the crown) and these break down naturally. You can of course collect your leaves and create your leaf mould, which, although not rich in nutrients, is very good at improving the soil structure and can also be added as a mulch. I go into more detail about leaf mould and homemade compost in Chapter 8.

If you are adding a mulch bought from a nursery or retailer, it is very important to make sure that it doesn't contain any peat. The ban on peat-based products is slowly making progress, but there are still a lot of composts and soil conditioners out there that do still contain peat. Companies are working on alternatives to peat, and it is a case of finding a product that you like to work with. The world's peatlands are of enormous importance to the planet as they capture huge amounts of carbon which has a net cooling effect on the atmosphere and in turn this will help to reduce the overall warming of the planet. So, it is vitally important that we don't continue to deplete these very important areas by removing the peat for commercial purposes.

Avoiding compaction is another important step to healthy soil. It is therefore best to avoid walking on your borders too often. I have used stepping stones to allow me to move around the border when I am deadheading or weeding. I also have access to the borders from both sides, so I can work from each side to avoid having to walk on the soil. I know this isn't always possible for everyone and it depends on how your garden space has been laid out. If you do find the soil compacted, you can gently hoe the top of the soil to loosen it up or take a border fork and break the surface of the soil up, being careful not to turn the soil of course. You can also use an old decking board or off cut of wood and lay it across the bed – standing on this will also reduce compaction when you are working in your borders or raised beds.

▨ Acidic and alkaline soil

You will often hear people say that they have alkaline soil or acidic soil, or maybe you have read the labels on new plants which say 'prefers a more acidic soil'. You may nod sagely but have only a vague understanding of what this means. If that is the case, and you are not the only person, here is a quick guide.

Plants that prefer more acidic conditions are happier in soil with a pH of less than 6.5 (soils with a pH less than 5.5 are classified as very acidic) and those preferring more alkaline conditions prefer a pH of 7.5 or over. A pH of between 6.5 to 7.5 is classed as neutral.

Some examples of plants which prefer acidic soils are Rhododendrons, Azalea and Pieris. Raspberries and blueberries also prefer acidic soil. If you do not have acidic soil and want to grow these plants and fruits, then you can add ericaceous mulch around and in the planting hole, which will help to reduce the pH of the soil in the area you have mulched, making it more hospitable to acidic soil loving plants. You will need to apply the mulch every year. If the leaves start to yellow, that is a sign that you need to increase the acidity of the soil. You can also buy ericaceous feed in granular and liquid form if you'd rather use these. I have my blueberries in pots and top up the pot every year with a layer of ericaceous compost. I also use an ericaceous liquid feed over the growing season. For my raspberries, I mulch with ericaceous compost at the start of the growing year and at the end of the year when I have cut the stems down. In summer, I give the raspberries a couple of liquid feeds. If you have shrubs in the ground that prefer acidic conditions, then I would use a mulch and give a couple of feeds using a liquid mix.

Carrying out a pH test will let you know what kind of soil you have. You can buy these from garden centres. I would recommend taking samples from different areas of your garden, as with climate conditions, you can also find that the pH levels can vary around the garden.

Alternatively, you can make your own pH test kit if you prefer. Here's how to do it.

Homemade pH testing kit

Equipment

- Trowel
- Two small containers (capacity over 250ml)
- A measuring cup (capacity around 250ml)
- Spoon
- Half a cup of white vinegar
- One cup of distilled water
- Half a cup of baking soda

Method

Fill both containers with soil from the area you wish to test. You can take some soil from different areas of the border and mix them in the container. Make sure that the soil is loose and you remove any stones or other debris.

To test for alkalinity, pour half a cup of distilled water into one container and mix with the spoon. Then add half a cup of white vinegar. If the mixture starts to fizz or bubble, then you have an alkaline pH.

To test for acidity, pour half a cup of distilled water into the second container and mix with the spoon. Add half a cup of baking soda to this. If the mixture starts to fizz or bubble, then you have an acidic pH.

If you want to make your soil more alkaline, you can add wood ashes or garden lime. And, if you want to increase the acidity of the soil, you can add pine needles, bracken leaves, or elemental sulphur.

If you have an established garden, it is worth noting down what plants thrive in your garden and when you are out for a walk, have a look at the type of plants that are doing well in your neighbour's gardens. This will give you a good idea of the type of plants that like the soil conditions that you have, although to be sure, I would always test.

▒ Top 7 takeaways from this chapter

1. Soil health is the foundation of a healthy garden, leading to plants that will thrive and crops that will flourish.

2. Don't disturb the structure of your soil, aim to get a good thick layer of topsoil.

3. Know your soil type and work with it. Make changes to improve its structure and nutrients.

4. Mulch, mulch, mulch – it really will pay you back in healthier plants, reduce the need for weeding, reduce evaporation and increase the biodiversity of your soil and garden.

5. Find out what the pH level of your soil is, that way you will know what type of plants will love to make a home there. Go on, get some samples and test your soil.

6. Don't use products containing peat, you really will be making a positive impact on the climate. Try out different products to see which ones work for you.

7. Avoid compacting the soil by walking over it, put in stepping stones or use boards when you are working in the borders.

Healthy soil is the foundation for a healthy garden; by taking some time to find out what soil you have, you will be on your way to having healthy plants and crops. In the next chapter, we will be looking at how we work with nature and examine how we can improve the environment around us to encourage more of it into our garden spaces.

Notes

_____

_____

_____

_____

_____

_____

_____

_____

_____

_____

_____

_____

_____

_____

_____

_____

_____

Chapter Three

Gardening Alongside Nature

"The glory of gardening: hands in the dirt, head in the sun, heart with nature. To nurture a garden is to feed not just the body, but the soul."

Alfred Austin

"The garden reconciles human art and wild nature, hard work and deep pleasure, spiritual practice and the material world. It is a magical place because it is not divided."

Thomas Moore

Choosing to not use chemicals such as herbicides, insecticides and pesticides is the only way to go if you want your garden and nature to survive and thrive. I have already discussed the importance of keeping the natural balance of soil because healthy soil will reward you with healthy plants. We should also apply this thinking to how we manage our gardens overall. I do not use any chemicals in my garden. I use my homemade compost to mulch, so using what has come from the garden goes back into the garden. That means that the nutrients, bacteria, and insects are all from the same area. I make my plant feed (other than ericaceous, I buy this in) from comfrey grown in my garden. More on how to make your compost and feed in Chapter 8. Everything in nature has a purpose and a job to do. Everything predates on or is predated on. If you use chemicals, you will upset this balance and harm the wildlife that visit your garden.

For example, the garden birds will come in and eat the aphids off of my roses, some will even take a slug or two. The bees and other pollinators will help to pollinate my fruit trees and soft fruit – their payment for this is delicious nectar. The hedgehog will eat the slugs and snails, as will the frogs, some bird species and ground beetles. Even wasps, often maligned, are welcome as they predate aphids. A lot of people think of insects such as aphids and slugs/snails as pests, but they have their own very important role in the garden. In the UK there are 44 species of slugs and out of that only nine species eat young plants. Slugs are very important to the ecosystem and are often referred to as the great recyclers of the garden. They will break down organic matter, which helps your compost heap and your soil health.

There are a lot of products out there that claim to prevent slugs and snails from reaching your plants. Never use slug pellets – they may be effective but can enter the food chain and affect those who prey on slugs and snails, like hedgehogs and birds. Making a garlic solution is reported to be very successful when sprayed onto your plants, but you will have to reapply after every rain shower. Other ways to deter slugs range from copper tape to eggshells, bran/oats and even sheep wool.

When you decide to garden with nature, you will feel so much better about everything you do in your garden. You will gain all the benefits when you sit and watch nature at work in your garden. Whether it's spotting how many pollinators you have buzzing around you, to how many small garden birds visit your garden. The hedgehog does his best to keep the numbers of slugs and snails down and the other garden birds can be seen in the fruit trees and roses feasting off bugs and caterpillars. But sometimes, you will get an infestation. You can use companion planting – this is where you have plants in your garden beds or vegetable beds which will either deter the unwanted bugs or will be so alluring to them that they will feed on this plant and not your other plants. I go into companion planting in more detail in Chapter 10.

The RHS has recently announced that it will no longer be referring to slugs, snails, aphids and caterpillars as pests. So, I won't either!

I don't personally use any sprays, I prefer to use companion planting and allow a good diversity of wildlife in the garden to stave off any infestations. But there are homemade sprays and preparations that you can make which can help to deter these insects from your plants. I have listed some of them below, along with how to make them.

▨ Homemade deterrents

Garlic spray

Take a whole garlic bulb, separate the cloves and remove the skin. Then chop the garlic finely by hand or use a blender along with 235 ml of water. Add another 700ml of water and around 30ml of liquid soap (castile soap is best). Blend or mix these and then put them in a jar, leaving this mixture to infuse overnight. Then strain the mixture to remove the pieces of garlic as they will block your sprayer. Add the mixture to your sprayer and you are ready to use the mixture. Keep this in the fridge between uses. Apply the spray to your plants; the liquid soap will help the mixture stick to the leaves. Repeat every couple of days or after any rainfall.

Black spot spray

In five litres of water, mix half a litre of milk and two tablespoons of bicarbonate of soda and add to a sprayer. Keep in the fridge between uses. Spray the leaves of plants liberally with this mixture.

Liquid soap spray

This spray is very effective at treating aphid, black fly and white fly infestations. Add liquid soap (castile soap is best) to water in a sprayer at the rate of 15 ml of soap to a litre of water. Spray the whole plant thoroughly; the aphids will be washed off and the soap will make the surface too slippery for them to land on.

Slug and snail deterrents

You can make a mix of chilli flakes and cayenne pepper and sprinkle this around your plants; you will have to renew this after rainfall. Crushed eggshells can be effective when placed around your plants; the slugs and snails won't like to move over the eggshells. Some people have found copper rings to be effective. I have used copper tape and have not found this to be much of a deterrent, unfortunately. Sheep wool placed around plants can also discourage slugs and snails as they can't move across this surface. You can also buy slug mats which you wrap around the base of your plants, these are impregnated with copper and some of my clients have found them to be effective.

Another way to deal with an infestation of slugs and snails is to reduce their habitat and therefore numbers. I built my raised vegetable beds out of branches and trunks of trees which had been felled – they looked lovely and very environmental. But I had not factored in that I had also created a perfect habitat for slugs and snails to live and reproduce in vast numbers! They lived in the gaps between the pieces of timber. So, even when I covered the seedlings with netting or cloches, they could attack from the sides! The solution is I have re-built the raised beds using decking boards, which are smooth and lock together tightly. I have surrounded the sides of the raised beds with copper tape. The copper tape has not been a huge success if I am honest and I probably won't renew it. I have employed the companion planting method to try and deter infestations – more about companion planting in Chapter 9. Companion planting has been very effective and also encourages pollinators. The polytunnel has two raised beds with copper tape surrounding them. I was hoping that the high temperatures and relatively dry atmosphere would deter the gastropods, but I can confirm that it hasn't, although the numbers are much lower than in the main garden and I just remove the slugs or snails when I see them climbing up the walls of the poly tunnel.

Netting and cloches are also useful and can keep them off of your seedlings until they are big enough to not be so appetising. I grow my vegetable plants from seed and don't put the plants out into the garden until I feel that they are big enough to survive being nibbled on. The strawberry plants are grown with landscape fabric covering the raised bed; this does deter the slugs and snails and it also means that the strawberry fruits are not sitting on wet soil.

▩ Hedgehogs

Get a hedgehog! I am not advocating going out actively to obtain a hedgehog – that would be cruel. But make your garden an inviting place for a hedgehog to come and visit or even stay in. Gary is our resident hedgehog. He started visiting our garden a few years ago and built a house for him. Instructions on how to build a hedgehog house can be found on the internet, or you can also buy ready-made houses from garden centres or nurseries. I can hear him snuffling about the borders and underneath the bird feeders at night.

He will sometimes grunt and will leave some poop which marks his territory. Esme, our dog, doesn't seem at all bothered by his presence in the garden, just giving him the side eye as she runs past him. He will feast on slugs and snails in the evening. The garden is surrounded by fencing so to allow him to visit other gardens I have cut a small hole at the bottom of a fence slat at the top and bottom of the garden. Our neighbours often report sightings of him in their gardens, which is a reassurance that he is still active. So far, he appears to live alone as there hasn't been any evidence of a second hedgehog or hoglets. It's just so nice to know that he has chosen our garden to call home.

▓ Frogs and toads

There are a couple of frogs in the compost heap – they don't have to go far for a meal! In the summer you see them on the top of the compost heap, and you have to be careful when you are adding anything to the heap – we don't want to drop anything straight onto them. They tend to move away when the carpet covering the heap is removed. As the weather cools, they burrow deeper into the heap to benefit from the warmth further down. I don't turn the heap as I don't want to cause any injuries from using the garden fork. But when it comes to moving the heap over to the new bay, a bucket is deployed and the frogs are removed by hand until the heap is moved and then they are gently put back on top of the heap.

Resident frog in the compost heap

Fungal infections

Another issue I have faced in the garden recently is brown rot on my Victoria plum tree. It has devastated my crops for two years. Brown rot is a fungal infection and pretty difficult to get the upper hand on. Your fruit will develop mouldy-looking spots and eventually turn brown and rot. You must remove any affected fruit that you see on the tree as well as any fallen fruit. I was doing this, but year two saw it return. So, what to do? Do not get out the herbicide!

With any fungal infection, you need to get rid of the infected fruit immediately, and I thought I had done a good job, but underneath my plum tree is a small area of vinca minor. Looks lovely, but hidden amongst the vinca was the fallen fruit I had not seen. As this is a fungal infection, the spores will live in the soil and come the next rain shower they lift and reinfect the tree. So, I reluctantly removed the vinca, cleared all the rotted fruit, put down a thick layer of cardboard (this is cardboard from delivery packaging) and covered that in a thick layer of bark mulch. The cardboard and bark should help to keep the spores from re-infecting the tree and I can now clearly see all the fallen fruit. I have pruned the tree to remove infected stems. I have also pruned it to make a more open shape rather like a goblet, which will increase the airflow – this again should help prevent the brown rot from taking hold. I do not want to lose the tree as it is so productive and is such a striking structural feature in the garden.

Update on the Victoria plum tree: my efforts have paid off and this year I had a really good harvest of healthy fruit. There were some infected fruits, but these were removed as soon as I saw them. I now do daily checks on the tree and at the base.

Similar steps can be taken to avoid black spot in roses. This is also a fungal infection. So, remove any fallen leaves and burn them or put them in your council brown waste bin. Please do not compost at home – home compost heaps will not reach high enough temperatures to kill off the fungal spores. Then remove any badly affected leaves from the rose itself. And, add a good thick layer of mulch around the base of the rose to keep the spores trapped. And finally, remember to prune your roses to increase the airflow in the plant. This means pruning to have an open structure, one where the stems are not crossing or crowding each other out. The shape you are looking for is a goblet shape. I will explain more about pruning techniques in Chapter 7. Black spot will not kill your roses but can be unsightly and it is always worth trying to break the cycle of the spores lying dormant in the ground.

So, as you can see, you can deal with many types of issues affecting your plants, trees, fruit or vegetables without resorting to chemicals. And remember, if you have healthy balanced soil, you will have much healthier plants and they will be better placed to fight off any attacks. It is worth taking a little time to work out what preventative methods you can take to minimise the damage that can be caused by infections or bug attacks.

▨ Birds

I love to watch the birds visiting the garden and the different songs of each species of bird. The sparrows arrive in a group of about 20, chattering as they swoop into the garden. They split up into groups: some go straight to the bird feeder, others are on the ground scrubbing for bugs, and others are in the fruit trees nibbling on aphids. While others take a drink and a quick dip in the bird bath. And without warning they lift into the air and switch positions; it is a sight to behold. You have to be careful if you are moving around the garden whilst they are doing all this as I feel them dart past my head, totally unfazed by my presence. Blue tits and great tits are also frequent visitors and will dart from the shelter of the Photinia red robin to the feeder and back. The chaffinch is very cautious and will sing his song, looking all around for predators before darting to the feeder. Sometimes I will spot a reed bunting and the shy wren can be heard but rarely seen. Blackbirds run across the lawn and move around the borders, finding insects to eat. The wood pigeon is ever present, sitting under the bird feeder and hoovering up fallen seeds.

But it was a different story when the garden was just a blank expanse of soil, no birds, no wildlife. Once the borders filled with plants and the trees and shrubs grew large enough to provide shelter from predators – there is a Sparrowhawk that visits the garden – the small garden birds started to visit the garden. They make around three trips to the garden every day, arriving at around 9 am, then early afternoon and just before dusk.

They find food in the bird feeders – I provide year-round supplies of sunflower hearts – and in the borders, where they will disturb the surface with their beaks to find insects and grubs to eat. The fruit trees and roses are also a great source of aphids, bugs and insects.

The birds will also bring their fledged young in the summer, so numbers increase quite dramatically as well as the noise level! It does give me such a thrill to see them and know that I have created a space that is as safe as I can make it for them and to be able to provide food for them that has not been touched by harsh chemicals.

I recently found an unused bird feeder in the shed and I have filled this with pieces of wool, some sheep's wool and dog fur. They will now be able to pluck these offerings from the old feeder and use it to make their nests.

Water

Water in the garden is also an important element in creating a nature-friendly space. I have shallow dishes placed around the garden and top these up with rainwater if the levels drop. I have placed some stones of different sizes in the dish, which are useful for small insects, butterflies and moths to perch on and get a drink. The birds and hedgehogs also benefit from these watering holes. I have a bird bath which is higher off the ground and is safe for the birds to drink from and bathe in. Again, I have different-sized stones in here to accommodate the smaller birds and insects. I only use rainwater to fill this up and I clean it out regularly. Creating a pond is also a great idea. You don't need to have a large space to create a pond. I have used a large tub, the bottom layer is made up of small stones, then I placed larger stones and cobbles working their way up to the surface. I have some pond plants in there including an oxygenator plant to keep the water clear – these are placed on bricks as they are more stable for the pots to sit on.

▓ Nesting box

A bird nesting box is also a must-have. I have a bird nesting box on the north-facing wall of the house. I have had three families of blue tits and two families of great tits that have been raised in the box. Again, it is joyous to see the little heads of the chicks looking out from the entrance hole. You can hear their cries for food as they sense their parents arriving with something to eat. Watching the parents in the back garden collecting bugs and aphids and flying down the side of the house to the nesting box at the front is mesmerising and heartwarming. I feel a certain amount of pride in being part of their lives. Once they fledge, the parents bring them into the back garden where I can watch them showing their young where to find the insects and bugs as well as the bird feeder. The bird nesting box came from the RSPB online store and they give you clear instructions on exactly where to place it and how high up it should be. I clean the nesting box in October each year, removing the old nest and then cleaning the inside of the box with very hot water, no chemicals. The nest itself is fascinating to look at, deep and spongy, made up of moss, wool, animal fur and dry leaves.

▓ Bug hotel

There is a bug hotel at the bottom of the garden; this was easy to build. I rolled a length of chicken wire into a tube shape and used three canes to weave into the wire; this keeps it closed and also acts as a support. I then added some dry leaves, dry twigs and finally some straw. It is in a quiet area of the garden, and to keep the worst of the rain off it, I have a piece of broken terracotta pot placed on top of the structure. I top this up every year with fresh straw and twigs. Now the small insects and bugs have somewhere to keep them safe, warm and dry when they need shelter.

▓ Sugar drink

Sometimes a sugar drink is just what the doctor ordered for our tired and thirsty pollinators. I was finding exhausted bees on the patio – they had run out of fuel. I knew that giving them a sugar drink would help get them buzzing again, but found that they fell into the saucer of sugar water that I was leaving out and they ended up a sticky mess. Here is an alternative way to provide the pollinators with an energy drink. Take an ordinary sponge with small holes in it, and place it in a shallow bowl. Make a sugar solution by filling a pot with water and adding sugar, bring to a boil and simmer until the sugar is dissolved. Once it is cool, add the sugar and water mixture to the bowl, soaking the sponge. Keep the solution in an old juice bottle to keep the bowl topped up. The tired pollinators can land on the sponge and suck up some of the sugar solution, recharge their batteries and fly off safely.

▓ Leave areas untouched

You can also leave areas in your garden untouched, and let the leaves and twigs gather. Insects can shelter or overwinter in these areas. Do not be too quick to tidy up the garden in winter; leave the stems of perennials and leave the seed heads on plants. Leave the cutting back until the last of the frosts in the spring, when any little visitors will have left the shelter of old stems or fallen leaves. If you have stems or small branches you can always make a habitat pile. You can add leaves and twigs to the centre of the pile. When creating this habitat pile, make sure the base is wider than the top, this will prevent it from toppling over or the wood from rolling off the pile. Insects and small creatures can shelter here over winter and once the wood starts to rot, it will become food for insects, worms and beetles.

▓ Weeds

There is a common saying that weeds are just plants in the wrong place. I am very happy to see that the conversation around weeds has opened up and people are becoming more accepting of what is termed a weed. I like to think of weeds as wildflowers – these are the original plants before we started producing cultivars and commercial plants. Many people are in favour of what is termed rewilding, which is a great discussion to start having. If you can leave an area of your garden to go wild and let nature do its thing, that is great. I am all in favour of this. But if you let this happen then you will find that some of the more dominant plants will take over and could crowd out other very useful wildflowers. Some examples of this are brambles, nettles and thistles, which, given the chance, will take charge of huge areas of land. So, I prefer to have a light touch approach and will remove any plants that are starting to take over, leaving room for the less boisterous to have a chance. After flowering, I also remove the seed heads, which will stop the spread of the plants around the garden. Yes, you may be removing some seed heads that the birds may have enjoyed, but if your garden is full of a variety of flowers that you leave the seed heads on, then the birds are being looked after. For example, a couple of years ago a teasel grew in the garden. This is a beautiful wildflower, statuesque, standing at around two metres tall. The pollinators loved the nectar, and the birds, especially the goldfinches, loved the seed heads. But, did this guy distribute a lot of seeds around the garden? I am still weeding the little seedlings out of the borders. You see, this particular plant is just too big and boisterous for the borders here, but I am quite happy for it to grow at the back of the garden and in the lawn. If you are happy to leave wildflowers to grow but don't want your whole garden covered in them, then I suggest deadheading or removing them after flowering.

▨ Lawns

There could be a whole chapter purely on whether we should or should not do anything with our lawns. There are debates currently over whether to let lawns go unmown, to water or not, and whether to apply fertiliser and weed killer. My personal opinion on this is that lawns are tough beasts and will survive a dry spell. Especially here in the UK where there may be long dry spells, but it does rain fairly frequently and the grass will recover very quickly. I just don't want to waste any precious water resources on the lawn.

I made the decision several years ago to stop fertilising and applying topical weedkiller. Thinking that I once did this, kind of makes me shudder. All of these chemicals go into the food chain and can only be destructive to wildlife. If you do want to feed your lawn, then a natural alternative is to use fish blood and bone granules or a seaweed fertiliser applied as a liquid soak. As to grass cutting, we are all getting more used to seeing areas left unmown in our community, whether it is parks or grass verges. To not mow the lawn is hugely beneficial to wildlife on so many levels. But most of us still need to use our lawns and perhaps would prefer to see our front lawns kept mown, but perhaps in the back garden we can try out different options. Here is what I do: I keep the edges sharp on my lawns. This helps keep the definition between the lawn and the border. I don't mow the lawn in certain areas and only cut this once in the autumn. These areas, rather grandly named lawn islands, have been planted with bulbs and wildflower plugs. This way, I still have access through the lawn but have areas left alone, so, for me, this is a good compromise. In fact, by leaving these small areas unmown, I have managed to attract a grasshopper to the garden. Isn't that wonderful?

Grass left unmown in the lawn with additional bulbs and wildflowers planted

Top 7 things to do to encourage and help nature

1. Do not use chemicals in your garden; they are not needed. Create a diverse habitat, work with nature and find solutions to any problems that you might encounter.

2. Leave areas 'untidy' and do not be too quick to cut back seed heads. Let an area of your garden become a wildflower spot.

3. Encourage a hedgehog into your garden, build a hedgehog house and make sure there is access in and out of your garden.

4. Put up a bird nesting box, but remember to clean it each winter.

5. Leave some of your lawn to grow long, plant some bulbs or wildflowers in your lawn.

6. Provide a sugar drink station for your pollinators.

7. Having some water in the garden, a bird bath or a shallow bowl is enough. Or make your small wildlife pond. Put stones in shallow dishes for the butterflies!

Being more aware of nature around us, how we impact it and what we can do to improve it, are the key elements that we have looked at in this chapter. I hope that you have found it useful and that you are already thinking of some changes you want to make. We don't have to fight nature, we are nature, and we must all work together. The next chapter will look at hardiness zones and map the climate zones in your garden, which all goes to help get the right plants in the right place.

Notes

_____

_____

_____

_____

_____

_____

_____

_____

_____

_____

_____

_____

_____

_____

_____

_____

_____

_____

Chapter Four

Climate Maps and Hardiness Ratings

"The garden suggests there might be a place where we can meet nature halfway."

Michael Pollan

"If you wish to make anything grow, you must understand it, and understand it in a very real sense."

Russell Page

Beth Chatto, one of Britain's foremost and influential gardeners, had a mantra that was 'right place, right plant'. How true this is: if you have a very dry garden and you try to grow something like a damp-loving fern or Hosta, then it will not do well. You may love them, but if you do not have the right conditions for the plant then it will not flourish or even survive. If you like a particular plant but do not have the right conditions in the garden, look for a plant with similar attributes that will tolerate the conditions. For example, I love lavender, but my soil is too heavy and nutrient-rich, so they just do not grow well. I grow nepeta instead. It has a heady scent and gorgeous purple flowers which billow above a compact crown. It looks great planted as an individual specimen in a mixed border, but also looks great as an edging plant and planted en masse. The bees love this plant and the sound of their buzzing can be heard from some distance away. I grow it in a long row in the front garden which gets morning and evening sun (it is north-facing so isn't sunny enough for lavender) and it looks amazing. I get the effect I wanted from lavender but from a different plant which is happy in the conditions.

▨ Climate maps

A climate map is a visual reference showing the growing conditions in a garden space throughout the year. I am a pencil and paper person, so I would get my notebook out and sketch the layout of my garden. You can also use any number of apps or online garden design tools that are available.

If you have recently inherited a garden, then you will build up your climate map information over the year as you observe where the sunny spots are, the drier areas, and where water pools or ice pockets are in winter. If you know your garden well, then you will already have an idea of the different climate zones within your garden, but this will give you a chance to observe and note down key climate information.

If you have tested your soil, you can note down the pH levels in each area of the garden. Your soil type is likely to be similar around the garden, but you should note down if there are areas of compaction, free draining, poor or good soil quality. In my garden the soil type is clay, but it is less free draining at the bottom of the sloped area as this is where the water can pool. I also note where there is shade from trees and large shrubs as well as where there are likely to be pockets of frost in the winter months. You should also mark down where you have paths, patios or structures such as a shed or greenhouse.

Here is my guide to creating your climate map.

Creating a climate map of your garden

- Draw the boundaries of your garden.
- Mark out the areas of hard surfaces such as patios and paths.
- Now put in any structures in the garden, sheds or polytunnels for example.
- If you have a lawn, then mark this area down.

- Now identify where north is and mark this with an arrow pointing north, I add an N just to be very clear!
- Mark where the sun comes up and where the sun sets today – but be aware that this will change with each season. You can now track the movement of the sun as the day progresses.
- As the sun moves during the day, note where the shading occurs and for how long the shade is there. So, one area may be in the shade in the morning only, for example; note this down.
- You may want to note the difference in light levels for each of the seasons. For example, the area at the very bottom of the garden only gets sun in the late afternoon in the winter months, but in spring and summer, the sun hits that area in the morning and early afternoon through to evening.
- Are areas in the shade because of large trees or shrubs?
- If the ground slopes, draw this in and mark which way the slope goes.

- Mark the drier areas and then the areas where the soil is wetter.
- Are there areas that are prone to flooding or pooling of rainwater?
- What direction is the prevailing wind coming from?
- In winter and spring, where are the cold spots, the areas that get the most frost?
- You have discovered your soil types – are all the areas the same or should you mark where the soil is different?
- If you have tested your soil, mark down what the pH levels are in the different areas of the garden.
- Where are the areas of high traffic, that is, areas where people tend to walk, or children play?

Once you have created a climate map of your garden space you will have a clear visual guide, allowing you to identify where plants will do best. If you are buying plants, you can now choose plants that will suit the site you want to put them in, plants that will have a better chance of survival and will perform at their best in the right conditions. You are now armed with the knowledge of your soil type and structure, and the climate conditions, making it easier when choosing the right plant for the right place. A climate map is also very helpful if you are thinking of re-designing your garden space. More about this in Chapter 10.

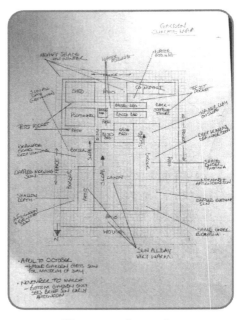

Climate map of my garden

Hardiness ratings

In the UK the hardiness ratings are split into seven, ranging from H1 to H7, and refer to the hardiness of plants rather than using geographical zones. I live in Central Scotland near the coast, and I can safely grow plants with a hardiness rating of H4 to H7 outside without protection. Plants with a hardiness rating of H3 to H2 can be grown outside and given some protection over the winter and have a good chance of survival. H1-rated plants will grow outside during the summer months but will need to be brought inside to overwinter.

There will be a label on any plants you buy from nurseries or garden centres – the hardiness rating of the plant will be marked on this label. You can also check the RHS website, which will give you information on the particular requirements of your chosen plant including its hardiness rating. If you do buy something that isn't hardy enough to be outside in the winter, you can still grow it, but bring it inside or into a sheltered area when the temperatures drop. It is possible to grow, say, a lemon tree in certain parts of the UK, but it will need protection over the winter.

H1a

You can move these plants outside during the summer months if the temperature is 15 degrees or higher. Any lower than this, you will have to bring them inside into a heated environment under glass. If the temperature is fluctuating, it may be best to bring them under cover, either in a greenhouse or the house.

H1b

The lowest temperature that the plants in this category will survive is 10 degrees. As with H1a plants, these plants need consistency in temperatures and may benefit from being grown indoors or under glass if the weather conditions are changing.

H1c

Bedding plants tend to come under this rating and can be grown outdoors during the summer months in most areas of the UK. The minimum temperature that these plants will tolerate is five degrees Celsius.

H2

These plants are described as tender and will need unheated protection over the winter months as they won't tolerate frost. This can be in a greenhouse, polytunnel or cold frame. The minimum temperature for this group of plants is one degree Celsius.

H3

The plants in this category can be described as half-hardy in that they can survive outdoors in milder areas of the country but will be at risk from early frosts. They can also be damaged or killed in cold winters unless given some protection, such as a fleece covering or being placed in an unheated greenhouse or cold frame. They can survive in temperatures down to minus five degrees Celsius.

H4

This covers plants described as hardy and will survive outside during a cold winter with temperatures as low as -5 to -10 degrees Celsius. In very exposed areas you may get some frost damage to leaves.

H5

These are also described as hardy plants which will survive a cold winter in temperatures down to -10 or -15 degrees Celsius. Again, in a prolonged frost, you may find that some leaves are damaged by the low temperatures.

H6 to H7

This range covers plants that will survive in temperatures as low as -20 degrees Celsius. Very unusual for the UK, but there will be areas of the country that may experience this.

▓ Top 7 takeaways from Chapter Four

1. Get a pencil and notebook to start your garden climate map. Draw where your garden boundaries are.

2. Note down which way is north, where the prevailing winds come from, which areas are frosty in winter and spring, and whether

there are any areas that are prone to flooding or drying out.

3. Mark down where you have paths, patios, sheds or other outbuildings.

4. Where are the sunny spots in the garden and at what time of day? Where are the shaded areas? And at what time of day does the shading occur?

5. If the garden is new to you, take notes every month so that you get an all-round understanding of the garden climate throughout the seasons.

6. When choosing plants for your garden, remember to check the hardiness rating for that plant – will you have to provide winter protection or can it survive the lowest temperatures in your garden?

7. If the climate of your garden doesn't suit the plant you want, look for an alternative that gives you the same look and feel but will thrive in the conditions you have.

We can't predict a very cold winter, but armed with your climate map, you will have a clear idea of where the hot spots and, more importantly, the cold spots are in your garden. If you do grow plants in pots and they can be left outside, it is useful to tuck them into a sheltered area and provide some protection over the winter. And, if you are investing in new plants, make sure that they are suited to your local winter conditions. Equally, there will be alternatives if the plant you want isn't suitable for your growing conditions.

Notes

_____

_____

_____

_____

_____

_____

_____

_____

_____

_____

_____

_____

_____

_____

_____

_____

_____

Chapter Five

Growing Flowering Plants From Seed

"Flowers always make people better, happier and more helpful; they are sunshine, food and medicine for the soul."

Luther Burbank

"You have to get up and plant the seed and see if it grows, but you can't just wait around, you have to water it and take care of it."

Bootsy Collins

Why grow flowering plants from seeds? Well, for me, it is the buzz of it! The thrill of taking a seed from a packet, sowing it and watching it grow into a mature plant ready to go out into the garden never fades. I promise you that you too will get the same pleasure and satisfaction of having plants in your garden that you have grown from seed. It is also much cheaper to buy a packet of seeds than a plant from a nursery. I am not advocating that you don't buy a perennial or annual plant from your local nursery, but there is a thrill that you get from growing something from seed yourself which is very different from the excitement of buying from a nursery or garden centre. I think like everything in life, a bit of a mix-and-match approach seems to work well for most people.

Let's just talk about seed shopping first and get it out of the way. Now, I do not think I am the only person who has overbought on the seed front. The catalogues and websites are so tempting, aren't they?! I order what I think are a few packets and then when they all arrive, I am always astounded and exclaim, I didn't order all of this! Now, I have been in this cycle for many years with vegetable seeds. They do get used up and I always distribute them to friends and family. But in more recent years, I have started to look longingly at the perennial and annual seed packets. Could I possibly grow these plants from seeds? Well, the answer is yes, I can, and I have many plants in my garden to prove it. But so buoyed by my success, I have started to overorder these as well as my vegetable seeds. I have had to upgrade my small seed shoe box to a larger wooden seed box. But I must not go any bigger...ok. Anyway, enough about my seed purchasing issues.

I am going to take you through how to sow and germinate seeds, but before that, I am going to explain the difference between half-hardy annuals, hardy annuals, biennials and flowering perennials. It is important to know the difference between them as it will determine how and when you sow your seeds. So, let's look at each one separately.

■ Half-hardy annual

These are plants which grow, flower, set their seeds and die in one year. This group of plants are usually the showy, large and very glamorous flowering plants. They will not generally survive the winter in the UK. You should leave the flower heads to go to seed and collect the seeds if you want to grow the same plant in the following year, or you can buy more seeds. More about seed collection in Chapter 6. If you are not collecting the seeds, you can just dig these plants up at the end of the year and put them in your compost heap or your garden waste bin.

Some examples of half-hardy annuals are:

- Cosmos
- Calendula
- Nicotiana
- Zinnia

- Tagetes
- Sunflower
- Antirrhinum
- Cobaea
- Cleome
- Amaranthus

▨ **Hardy annual**

These also flower, set their seeds and die in one year. The difference between these and the half-hardy annuals is that they can be germinated outdoors. Their seeds will survive outdoors (unless it has been a particularly cold winter) and should germinate again next year. Where you are in the UK, how sheltered your garden is and what type of winters you experience, are the factors which will determine if the seeds will germinate again giving you flowers for another year. These plants will flower all the way through to the first frosts when you can dig them up and put them in your compost heap or garden waste bin. As with the half-hardy annuals, you can also collect the seeds from these and use them in the following year.

Some examples of hardy annuals are:

- Poppy
- Nasturtium
- Vipers Bugloss
- Orlaya grandiflora
- Nigella
- Linaria maroccana
- Ammi majus
- Cornflower
- Larkspur
- Alyssum

■ Flowering perennials

Flowering perennial plants will die back at the end of the autumn and regrow every spring. They have a slightly shorter flowering season than the annual plants. There are so many varieties of perennials to choose from and there is a perennial for every garden climate. You can buy flowering perennials as potted plants which you can plant straight into your borders or pots, or you can choose to grow them from seed. This is the method we are looking at in this chapter. You can also increase your stock of perennials by lifting and dividing mature perennials and replanting them in other areas of the garden. I go into this method in more detail in Chapter 6.

Some examples of perennials are:

- Ornamental grasses
- Leucanthemum
- Scabious
- Astrantia
- Erigeron
- Aquilegia
- Geum
- Silene
- Delphinium
- Lupin
- Dianthus

▇ Biennials

These flowering plants produce roots, stems and leaves in their first year and then flower, drop their seeds and die in their second year. If left undisturbed their seeds will germinate in the spring of the following year producing the roots, stems and leaves and so the cycle continues.

Some examples of biennial plants are:

- Primula
- Evening primrose

- Sweet Rocket
- Hollyhocks
- Angelica
- Forget-me-not
- Honesty

Let's get sowing some seeds...

Seed sowing

Equipment

Below is a list of the equipment that you will need to have ready when you sow your seeds. I have listed different types of trays or modules that you can use, but this list is not exhaustive – gardeners are very inventive people who like to recycle and find uses for items rather than throw them away! My garden mantra is: "That will come in useful one day"! I have kept the plastic modular trays that some shop-bought annuals came in – these work very well when it comes to potting on the growing seedlings. I also keep the trays that shop-bought mushrooms come in. I pierce holes into the bottom and it instantly becomes a seed tray. The larger of these trays can also be used as the bottom water trays. You can also use the cardboard tube from a toilet roll or old yoghurt pots as vessels to sow your seeds into. Just remember to put some holes in the trays or pots for drainage. Coir pellets are also very good; coir is a growing medium like compost which is compressed to produce a pellet. These are soaked, they swell and then you plant the seed into the pellet. Once the seedling is big enough to put into a larger pot, you just plant the seedling and coir pellet as one, this is also true of coir pots.

- Seed tray, modular seed tray, coir pellets or pots
- Bottom water tray
- Seedling compost – unlike potting compost this is low in nutrients and has very good drainage
- Watering can with rose attachment or a plant mister
- Your seed packet
- Plant label and pen – you can also use old lollipop sticks as a label
- A plastic bag and something to tie the bag closed or a zip-lock freezer bag will also work
- Perlite – this can be added to your potting compost to help with drainage and is optional
- Fine grit or vermiculite – this can be used to cover the seeds instead of using potting compost and is optional

Seed sowing equipment showing a modular seed tray, a seed tray, water tray, compost, seeds, plant label and pen

Method – sowing the seeds

When you buy your seeds, the packet will give you guidelines as to when to sow, how to sow, how deep to sow and when to plant out into the garden. It is very tempting, and I am very guilty of this, when you get the first light and warm days of March, to rush to my seed packets and start sowing. Only for frosts to come and sowings are more often than not unsuccessful. Or if they are successful, when they are ready to be planted out, the weather still isn't warm enough for them. It is better to wait. Your seed packet will give you guidelines on the best time to sow indoors or in a greenhouse and outdoors directly into the soil. Of course, you should also bear in mind that this is guidance only, as where you live and the weather conditions will vary. As I have said, I live on the east coast of Scotland which is colder than say the southeast coast of England. So, I will be sowing a little later, normally 3-4 weeks later than the earliest recommended date on a seed packet.

So that I don't overcomplicate this section, I will refer to a seed tray, but this could be any tray or pot that you have chosen to use. A modular seed tray has been divided into sections rather than one complete tray.

Fill the seed tray with your seedling compost – this compost is loose and free-draining but isn't high in nutrients. You don't want compost with high levels of nutrients as you will just get some very quick but weak growth. It is at the next stage that you need to use some nutrient-rich potting compost. I also add some perlite to my compost, which aids with water retention. This is optional; you will get results from just using the seedling compost, but this for me is belts and braces! Once you have filled your seed tray, just even out the surface and gently firm the compost. Using your watering can (with rose attachment) gently soak the compost. If you soak the compost now, you will avoid the small seeds from moving around after watering.

Now get your seeds and put them on top of the compost. If I am using a modular seed tray, I will usually sow two or three seeds per module in case some don't germinate. If I am using a seed tray, then I sow the seeds very thinly over the top of the soil. Larger seeds can be placed individually, but if you are sowing small seeds, just sprinkle thinly. Then lightly press the seed using the back of your hand – this makes sure that the seed has contact with the compost. Now you can add a very fine layer of compost, grit or vermiculite on top of the seed and compost. The seed packet will give you guidance on how deep the seed should be under the surface of the soil. Generally speaking, the smaller the seed the less it needs to be covered by compost. I have found that either of the other suggested mediums (grit, vermiculite) have worked equally well.

Always label your seed trays. I use a wooden label and a waterproof marker pen or pencil, but you can use plastic labels or old lollipop sticks. The advantage of the wooden label is that it can be composted. However, plastic labels can be reused if you remove the previous writing.

I now use a plant mister to gently moisten the top of the seed tray – not too much as you don't want to risk the seeds rotting. If you are using a bottom water tray, you can also put the water into here and it will be soaked up by the compost.

Cover the seed trays using clear plastic bags and ties. You can also use pieces of perspex or shatterproof glass – I have kept the glass shelves from an old fridge for this purpose. Doing this creates a greenhouse effect. The air around the seeds is kept moist and warm, which helps with germination, especially if the evenings are still a bit chilly. I remove the bags once the seeds have germinated.

Place your seed trays somewhere warm and with natural light. This can be on a warm windowsill in your house. A heated greenhouse or propagator is ideal or a polytunnel when the weather warms up.

I am lucky enough to now have a polytunnel which allows me to put my seedlings in there from around mid-April. I like to wait until the temperature in the polytunnel is around ten degrees Celsius during the day. If there is a frost forecast, I will cover the seedlings with some fleece overnight. I also make use of windowsills in my house to germinate seeds. I have a small greenhouse, around 1.5m high with two shelves, and I also have a 2m high half greenhouse (in that it sits against a fence and has front doors and two hinged top opening lids) which has three shelves. These are useful and do not take up a lot of space, and also help to house some of the plants that are just not quite big enough to go into the garden yet. I understand that buying any of these can be an expense as you start, but growing on your windowsill is a very efficient way to start seedlings off.

Young seedlings in the polytunnel

Potted on seedlings in the small greenhouse

Sowing directly into borders and pots

Some seeds are best sown directly into their final position, that is in your border or pots. They don't like to be disturbed by pricking out and potting on. If you are sowing directly into your borders, then make sure that the area is weed-free, and the surface of the soil is not compacted. Loosen it up a bit using a hand fork. Water the area you are going to seed, let the water drain away and then sprinkle your seeds lightly. You do not want to overcrowd the seedlings, although you can always thin them out once they germinate. Lightly cover the seeds with soil or fine grit. If you use grit to cover your seeds, then you have a visual reminder of where you have broadcast your seeds. I would always mark where I have sown the seeds, as it is easy to forget the exact location and then wonder if the seedlings are weeds or not. Keep the soil moist until the seeds germinate.

If you are using a pot to sow your seeds into, then make sure that there is good drainage, add your compost and firm this lightly with your hand. Water the compost at this stage. Sprinkle your seed over the compost and pat the seeds down to make sure there is contact with the soil. Cover lightly with compost, vermiculite or fine grit. Keep the compost from drying out.

Germination

You should see some signs of germination: small dots of green will appear at the surface of the soil as the young stem pushes up towards the light. This will normally be around 2-3 weeks after sowing your seeds. The first leaves to appear are the cotyledon or seed leaves. These leaves cannot photosynthesise (see Chapter 1 for the definition of photosynthesis) but have stored energy within them to start the process of growing the stem and producing the true leaves. The seed leaves will soon be followed by the true leaves – these leaves will look generally like the adult leaves of the plant – and now the process of root growth begins in earnest. Once you see the true leaves you know that roots are starting to form. It is at this point, when there is a decent amount of seedlings that have germinated, that I remove the plastic bag covering the seed tray. This is to avoid the leaves rotting when they come into contact with the bag. It will then be almost time to pot these little gems on.

Pricking out and potting on

Your seedlings now have their true leaves, they will have a short sturdy stem and the seed tray they are currently in will start to look quite crowded.

A crowded seed tray. Seedlings are ready to be potted on

Their new roots will now be looking for some nutrition, they've used up the sugars in the cotyledon leaves and the seedling compost will not be nutrient-rich. This is now the stage where you should be planning on removing the seedlings from the seed tray; the term used is pricking out. Have your pots ready and filled with potting compost beside you before you start to prick the seedlings out. The pots you choose shouldn't be too big, I use pots that are around 9cm. Fill these with potting compost and make a deep hole in the middle. The roots can't be exposed for too long as they could dry out. Then take something like a pencil or chopstick and insert this carefully into the compost beside the first seedling. To remove the seedlings safely, only ever hold a leaf, usually the seed leaf, and never hold the stem. If the leaf breaks, the plant will produce another leaf, but it only has one stem. Gently hold one of the leaves and using the pencil loosen the soil around the seedling. Don't pull on the seedling – if it isn't coming out of the soil easily, keep loosening the soil around the roots. Now, gently lower the seedling into the hole you have created in the compost. Do not firm it in; I just give the pot a gentle tap on top of my potting table. The soil will settle around the stem. If you firm the seedling in you may damage the stem or roots, and they are very fragile at this stage. I water from below as I do not want the leaves to get wet and rot. I place the 9cm pots back in the bottom water tray and then add water to the tray; the seedlings will soak up the water from below. Again, you do not want the soil to completely dry out, but you definitely do not want to over water. If you water from below, the plant only takes up what it needs.

If you have used coir pellets, coir pots or toilet roll tubes to sow your seeds into, then you can put these directly into your larger pots and surround them with potting compost.

Remember to label your pots! If you are growing more than one type of plant, it is very easy to get them mixed up – or as I have been known to do, forget what I have planted!

As you are growing your seedlings indoors or under cover, they aren't being exposed to outdoor weather conditions. So, to get nice strong stems on your seedlings you should sweep your finger across them, back and forth. This mimics the wind passing over the stems and encourages the stems to grow stronger to stand up to windy weather.

Pricking out seedlings ready to pot on into 9cm individual pots

Removing seedlings carefully before placing them into the 9cm pots

Placing the seedlings into 9cm pots

Ready for the garden

You've sown your seeds, you have watched them burst through the compost and germinate. You now have healthy seedlings which you have potted on into individual pots. The time for getting these little plants out and into your garden is approaching, you are getting nearer to enjoying seeing the plants flower in your borders or pots. It's exciting, but when are they ready for the garden?

Harden off your plants – your little plants have been grown indoors or under cover, so you don't want to take them straight from this controlled environment to the more unpredictable one outdoors. Hardening your plants involves taking them outdoors during the day and bringing them back indoors at night. Doing this helps to acclimatise your young plants. This is normally carried out a couple of weeks before putting them into the garden. If you have a cold frame (cold frames are situated outside, normally with a wooden frame and lid which can be open during the day and closed at night) then place the plants in here and close the frame at night.

The weather conditions will very much dictate when you put the plants out into the garden. If the weather is warm enough for the particular plant you are growing, check your seed packet and follow their guidelines. But as we discussed in Chapter 4, keep in mind the climate particular to your garden. If the weather is yet to warm up where you are, then continue to harden your plants off until the temperature rises. I always wait until the last late-night frosts have happened – which can be well into May sometimes. Better to be cautious than to have your young plants affected by a frost.

A healthy root system is key to ensuring the success of your plant once it is outside in the garden or in a pot. How do you know if the root system is good and strong? Have a look at the bottom of the pot: can you see roots emerging from the drainage holes in the pot? You can also gently tip the plant out of the pot. To do this, I place my palm over the top of the pot, with my fingers on either side of the plant, then tip the pot upside down. If you can see roots around the edges of the compost and the compost doesn't fall away, then you are ready to plant out.

Delay planting out if the weather isn't quite warm enough, there are still overnight frosts, or the root system needs a bit more time to develop. However, if the leaves start to yellow, then this is a sign that the plant has used up all the nutrients in the potting compost. If this is the case, you can pot the plant on again into a slightly larger pot whilst you wait until the plant and the weather are ready.

*Checking for healthy root growth – roots can
be seen growing through the soil*

*A healthy root system on this seedling is visible
when you remove the plant from the pot*

Onion and shallot seedlings planted into the raised bed

Top 7 key points when sowing from seed:

1. Always read the instructions on the seed packet carefully to establish when and how to sow the seeds. Keep the seed packet for reference as you grow the plant.

2. Don't rush to sow your seeds if the weather isn't warm enough – you will end up with poor germination and weaker plants.

3. Have your equipment ready and close at hand when you start to sow the seeds, prick out the seedlings and pot them on.

4. Make sure that the compost doesn't dry out, but don't overwater or the seeds will rot.

5. Make your own greenhouse using clear plastic bags and ties. Once your seeds have germinated, remove the bags.

6. When you are ready to pot the seedlings on, use a pen or chopstick to loosen the soil around the seedling and handle only the leaves and not the stem.

7. Make sure the weather is warm enough and that there is a good root system before planting out into the border or pots.

Growing your own flowering plants from seed is very satisfying and I am sure once you have had one success, you will be hooked. There are other ways to increase your flowering plant stock and we will look at these methods in Chapter 6.

Notes

_____

_____

_____

_____

_____

_____

_____

_____

_____

_____

_____

_____

_____

_____

_____

_____

_____

_____

Chapter Six

Propagation

"If you've never experienced the joy of accomplishing more than you can imagine, plant a garden."

Robert Brautt

"I grow plants for many reasons: to please my eye or to please my soul, to challenge the elements or to challenge my patience, for novelty or nostalgia, but mostly for the joy of seeing them grow."

David Hobson

Propagation is the term used to describe increasing your plant stock using a parent plant to provide the means to duplicate the original. Growing from seed is just one way of doing this, but there are many other ways to do this, and in this chapter I will look at some of these other methods.

When we moved to our current house, the garden was just an expanse of soil. I had brought some plants from my old garden and they sat huddled in the corner until I had sketched out the basic layout of the garden. When I placed these plants around the garden, it became very clear that I needed a lot more plants if the borders were going to look even half full! Even now, 14 years later, the garden is still evolving and I am always looking for ways to increase my plant stock. I also like to give any surplus plants, cuttings or seeds away to friends who are looking for some new plants. I have used different methods to get more of a particular plant or shrub. For example, I have a particularly nice Cornus flaviramea and had spaces where this would add some good winter stem colour. I took softwood cuttings from the parent plant to create new plants. A perennial that is equally as good for propagating is my sedum autumn joy (or as it is known now Hylotelephium spectabile herbstfreude – rather a mouthful!) as this divides very easily and I have it dotted around the garden, all for the cost of the original plant.

Let's look at the various ways that you can increase your plant stock.

Softwood cuttings

Softwood cuttings are taken in the summer when the new growth of that year is, as the name suggests, still soft and can be easily bent. These types of cuttings usually have a very high success rate. You can take softwood cuttings from perennials such as Penstemon, Pelargonium, Verbena and Achillea. And these shrubs: Cornus, Buddleia, Hydrangea and Fuchsia.

It is best to take these cuttings in the morning before the day really heats up and the moisture levels in the plant will still be high.

It is very important to plant these cuttings as quickly as you can, so it is important to have everything prepared before you go out and collect your cuttings.

Equipment

- A sharp knife or secateur
- A plastic bag or freezer bag
- Small pots, 9cm or 11cm will do
- Potting compost
- Pencil
- Plant labels and pen
- Watering can

Method

Take your secateurs/knife and your plastic bag over to the plant that you want to take cuttings from. You want to choose a nice straight non-flowering stem or shoot. A stem of around 5-10 cm or 2-4 inches is the ideal length. Now, cut just above a bud on this stem. Put this immediately into your bag and seal the bag. The reason for putting the stems into the sealed bags is that they will lose moisture as soon as they have been removed from the parent plant. If you put them into the bags, then you are giving yourself time to collect more cuttings and take them back to where you are going to pot them up. You are now able to go around the garden collecting your cuttings.

When you have all the cuttings you need, go back to where you are going to pot up. Everything is ready to go and you should only take out one stem at a time, and seal the bag up until you are ready to prepare the next cutting.

Take your cutting and cut below a leaf node, cut straight across – this will be the bottom of your cutting. Remove all the lower leaves and pinch out the growing tip. The growing tip is the fresh new growth that you can see at the very top of the cutting normally between the last two leaves.

Fill your pot with compost and use a pencil or something similar to make a hole for the cutting to go into. I do this around the edge of the pot. Leave about an inch between the cuttings. You can now water the pots, but make sure the rose is attached to your watering can so that you water these stems gently.

As always, remember to label your cuttings. I have been guilty of thinking that I will remember exactly what cutting is in which pot, and invariably I have forgotten! So, always label.

To create a humid atmosphere which allows the cutting to take root and eventually produce new growth, cover with a plastic bag and tie the bag with string or an elastic band. You will know when the cutting has rooted because you will see new leaf growth on the stem and you can remove the plastic bag.

Leave these to carry on growing bigger and stronger and pot on until they are ready to be put into the garden. You may feel that they are ready to go into the garden in the autumn, or might want to leave until the following spring to plant them out. I would leave until the following spring to give them the very best chance to survive. I will put these plants in the small unheated greenhouse or the polytunnel during the winter months. If you have enough cuttings of a particular plant, you can try putting half of them out in the autumn and leave the other half until the spring.

Whichever time you choose to plant these out, you will have to harden them off first. This applies to anything that has been grown on a windowsill, in a greenhouse or polytunnel. To harden off simply means to put the plants out during the day and bring them in at night. Do this for 1-2 weeks and then you will be able to leave them out, in a sheltered spot, both day and night, and then they are ready to be planted in the border.

▨ Hardwood cuttings

You can take hardwood cuttings of shrubs, trees and climbers in the autumn and winter months. The cuttings come from the growth that has been put on over the current year. The growth will be less supple than that of softwood cuttings.

Cuttings can be taken from shrubs such as Buddleia, Cornus, Forsythia and Philadelphus. The climbing Honeysuckle is also a good candidate for hardwood cuttings. Trees such as willow are successfully propagated from hardwood cuttings.

Like the softwood cuttings, you are best to prepare for the arrival of the cuttings and have the following ready.

Equipment

- A sharp knife or secateur
- A plastic bag or freezer bag

- Small to medium-sized pots
- Potting compost
- Pencil
- Plant labels and pen
- Spade to dig a trench
- Compost and grit
- Watering can with rose

Method

Select only straight shoots as these will grow into a much better-shaped plant and cut a stem that is at least 12 inches long. Remove the soft growing tip, pinching out the soft new leaf growth at the top of the stem. Then take the long stem cutting and divide it into sections of around 15-30 cm or 6-12 inches in length. Lay these short sections side by side, noting which is the top of each stem. At the top of each stem make a slanted cut above a leaf node or a bud. You will now clearly see which is the top of the stem. As you do this more often, you will be able to see by eye how long you need the cutting to be, but until then you can use a pen or something that is around the right length to help you see where to make the next cut. Then cut the bottom of this straight across and do this below a leaf node or bud.

Using pots for your cuttings

If you are using a pot for your cuttings, select a square pot which is 9 cm or 11 cm in size. Fill the pot with potting compost and, using your pencil, make a hole in each corner of the pot. Now place the stem in this hole – remember the bottom of the stem has the straight cut – and bury it, leaving around one-third above the compost. Water and set aside in a greenhouse, cold frame or sheltered part of the garden.

Using the trench method for your cuttings

If you have room in your garden to try the trench method, then this is the least labour-intensive way of growing plants from hardwood cuttings. Select an area where the stem cuttings can remain for at least 12 months without disturbance. Using a spade, dig out a narrow trench that is around 9 inches deep. I put a little bit of homemade compost mixed with grit at the bottom of the trench, which will add nutrients and help with drainage. Insert the stems, straight cut at the bottom, leaving around a third of the stem above the soil. Push to soil around the stems, and water the area well.

When are hardwood cuttings ready?

You will know when the hardwood cutting has put down roots as you will see new leaf growth on the stem. If you have used the trench method, I would recommend that you leave the growing plants in the ground for at least 12 months, by which point they will have a well-established root system and be ready to be dug out of the ground and transplanted into the garden or a large pot. If you have grown the cuttings in pots, you should see some root growth coming through the drainage holes. If this is the case, then the cuttings are ready to be transplanted into larger pots. Have your larger pot to hand; this should be filled with compost and a hole created in the middle where you will place your cutting. Remove each cutting gently using your pencil or chopstick and carefully place this in the prepared pot.

▦ Layering method

The layering method for propagation purposes has a high success rate as the stem remains attached to the parent plant until there is good root growth on the layered stem. You can use this method on shrubs that have flexible stems and on stems that are near to the ground. You will possibly have noticed on some of your shrubs that this happens naturally in some plants. So, we are mimicking the natural habit of some shrubs. Examples of shrubs that are good for layering are Cotinus, Forsythia, Jasmine, Hazel and some Rhododendrons. You can also do this with raspberries and blackberries. My redcurrants do this naturally and I have many new plants that I have given away and some that I have kept in case the parent plant dies or is affected by disease.

The best time to carry out layering is in the spring and autumn. Layering works for both evergreen and deciduous shrubs, although spring is the best time for evergreen shrubs.

As always, it is better to get everything you need ready before you start to layer.

Equipment

- Cane or stick
- Twine
- Strong wire or U-shaped ground staple
- A sharp knife
- A small stick or piece of wood
- Watering can with rose

Method

Firstly, choose a flexible stem from the parent plant that is near the ground. Lay this stem along the ground, you will now push the cane or stick into the ground just slightly back from the end of the stem. This marks the point where the stem touches the ground.

Measure back around one foot from the end of the stem to a leaf bud. With a sharp knife, make an incision in the stem that goes through the leaf bud – but not through the stem – the incision should be around one inch in length. Use a small stick to keep this incision open.

Now create a shallow trench of about 10-15 cm or 4-6 inches deep which runs from just beyond the cut to the parent plant. Lay the stem in the trench and backfill the soil to cover the stem. Peg the stem down with the wire or the U-shaped ground staple – this will make sure that the stem will remain anchored to the soil. And now, this is where the cane comes in: take the end of the stem and bend upwards along the cane; tie this in with the twine. This will encourage the stem to have strong upward growth.

You should see a good root system developing in 12 months. When you do, cut the layered stem from the parent plant, remove the layered stem, being careful not to break the roots, and now you have your new plant. This can be placed in its new position immediately or potted up if you want to grow it to be a little bigger before planting out.

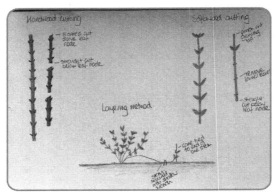

Illustration of hardwood and softwood cuttings and layering method.

▨ Lifting and dividing

If you grow perennials, then it is a good idea to lift and divide them every two to three years to keep the growth fresh and the flowering prolific. As perennials age, you can find that the centre can become quite sparse and you end up with all the growth and flowering around the outside. By lifting and dividing on a fairly regular basis, you will keep the vibrancy of the plant. If you are looking to increase your plant stock, you can lift and divide every year.

Examples of perennials to lift and divide

- ➢ Astrantia
- ➢ Leucanthemum
- ➢ Hosta

- Geranium
- Hesperantha
- Hellebore
- Rhubarb
- Rudbeckia
- Crocosmia
- Sedum

For example, my rhubarb was quite poor last year and it also flowered, which is a sign that the crown needed to be lifted out of the ground and divided. This will refresh the tubers and will encourage fresh new rhubarb shoots in the coming years. I also found that my sedum was starting to split and fall to the sides, a sure sign that it was getting just too big, so this was lifted and split into many new plants. Around 15 years ago I was given six primula vulgaris plug plants – these are our native primrose which you can see lining our roadsides and in our woods. A lovely plant for spring colour. Every few years I will dig up a good-sized plant, divide it into smaller plants and distribute them around the garden. So, from these six plants, I now have these special little plants all around the garden.

You can lift and divide perennials at any time of the year as long as you keep them watered afterwards in warmer weather. However, a simple rule of thumb is that for summer flowering plants it is best to do this in the spring and autumn. And for spring flowering plants you can do this after flowering in the early summer months.

Equipment

- A spade
- Two forks
- A saw or large sharp knife
- Watering can with rose

Method

Gently lift the plant out of the ground using a fork, and be careful not to damage the roots. You should loosen the soil around the plant but not too close to the edges of the plant. When the soil has been loosened around the plant, you can then push the fork underneath the plant and start to lift it out of the ground. If you meet resistance, then you haven't loosened the soil enough or dug deep enough down below the roots. Take your time and try not to rip the plant out of the soil. When the plant comes up, shake off the excess soil so that you can see the root system. Some plants, such as the primula, will have individual plants which you can tease apart. Some plants such as the sedum will pull apart quite easily and you should just divide up into smaller plants.

Other plants will have more fibrous roots, such as the Hemerocallis. This is where your two forks will come into play. Lay the newly dug-up plant on the ground and insert the forks back-to-back in the middle of the plant. Pull the forks apart using the handles and the plant will split in two. If you want to divide the plant again, then use this method on each of the smaller pieces.

Some plants will have tough roots or tubers and you will need a saw or large knife to cut through the roots to divide it up. I needed to use this method for my rhubarb.

Finally, with plants such as the Hellebore which have woody roots, it is best to use a spade to split the plant up. Lay the plant on the ground, place the spade in the middle of the plant and using your foot, press down on the spade and the plant will split.

You should replant as soon as possible to avoid the roots drying out. Dig a hole and plant to the same depth as it was originally. Give them a good soak and then mulch with compost. The plants may droop slightly for a few days, but they will bounce back quickly. If you are doing this in the summer months, keep an eye on them and water if you think they are drying out. If the divided plants have a lot of top growth and continue to droop, you can cut back this growth by around half. This will divert the plant's energy into establishing the roots and you will soon see re-growth above the surface.

▨ Buying established plants and trees

This is the most obvious method for increasing your plant stock and there are many places that you can buy new plants from. If you are starting your garden from scratch then this is your most likely source of plants, although friends and family are also a good source of plants and many people are only too happy to share their plants with you.

My friend recently moved into a newly built house and was establishing her garden from scratch. She had brought some plants from her previous garden and I had collected some plants from my garden to start the borders off. She used the local nursery to buy her shrubs and trees. Three years on the garden looks so well established and full of colour and texture. However, the cost of stocking the garden was reduced by reusing existing plants and being gifted plants propagated by me.

It is a thrill to go out and buy plants and if you follow these simple rules you will be spending your money wisely.

Buying from a nursery or garden centre

If you are using a local nursery, they will have a stock of plants suitable for every season, but they will also have seasonal displays of plants and it is useful to go throughout the spring, summer and autumn seasons to see the plants in that particular season. This is especially good if you are new to gardening or are not very familiar with certain types of plants.

You know the rule: never go food shopping when you are hungry? Well, I always say make a list of plants you are thinking of before going to the nursery as you may come away either having bought everything or bought only that particular season's plants. That is, if you go in spring without your list, you may come away with a lot of spring interest plants and nothing to cover the other seasons.

So, how do you come up with a list? In Chapters 2 and 4 we looked at knowing your garden's climate and soil type; this is your starting point. What plants are likely to grow well in your garden or a particular area of your garden? What season are you looking to have the plant look its best in? Ideally, your garden will have all year-round interest; I will go into more detail on this in Chapter 10. How many plants are you looking to buy? If you need a lot of plants, don't feel that you have to get them all in one visit; if it is easier just look for the number or type of plant you feel comfortable with. Some people start with just one plant, then add to them slowly.

Checking plant health

It is always important to check the health of the plant you want to buy at a nursery or garden centre. Check that there are no broken stems, that the growth looks lush and healthy and that there is a good root system. You should be able to remove the pot gently and check that the roots look healthy; if the pot doesn't come away easily or when it does the roots are very congested, then the plant is root-bound. This isn't a huge problem, but it means that the plant has been in the pot a little too long and the roots are going round and round. This is where, if you buy it, you tease the roots out before planting. If you don't do this the roots will continue to grow round and not outwards to find water and nutrients. If the soil falls away very easily, then the root system isn't very well established and the plant might struggle to establish itself when put into the ground.

Buying online

If you are buying plants online, then it is difficult to check the health of the plant before you purchase it and when it arrives. But always check the return policy if you do find that the plant arrives in a less-than-desirable state.

Buying bare-root plants

Another alternative is to buy bare-root plants from stockists online and through your local nursery. Bare root plants are available from around November to March – these are plants that have been grown in the ground and are lifted when they are dormant. If you are thinking of planting a new hedge, then buying your hedging as bare root plants is a very economical way to do this. You can also buy roses and fruit trees as bare-root plants which are much cheaper than buying them in pots. The plants will arrive as the name suggests with their roots exposed – as such it is really important to get them in the ground as soon as they arrive. They will be wrapped up to stop the roots from drying out, but they will dry out quickly. If you are not ready to plant them immediately, then you can pot them up, covering the roots with soil and giving them a good soak. You can also heel them into an area of the garden as a temporary home for them. To do this, create a trench and lay the plants in, cover the roots with soil and water. They will happily remain in this temporary home until their final placement. If you are ready to put the plants into their final position, then the process is the same as I have detailed below, but you should soak the roots in a bucket of water for at least an hour before you put them in the ground.

Whether you have purchased your plants from a nursery, garden centre or online, if you are not planting immediately, put them in a sheltered spot in the garden and make sure they are kept watered until you are ready to plant them.

When you are ready to put your plants in the ground, here is a quick guide to how to do this.

Equipment

- Bucket of water
- Spade
- Watering can with rose attachment
- Compost or mulch
- Tree stake and tie (if planting a new tree)

Method

When you are ready to get them in the ground, the first thing to do is soak the plants thoroughly. You can do this by watering from the top, but a more effective way is to get a bucket of water and place the plants (in their pots) into the water for an hour. Don't submerge the plant, just have the water cover the bottom of the pot.

Now you need to prepare the planting hole and dig a hole that is slightly wider and deeper than the root ball of the plant. Always plant to the same level as the plant was in the pot – the reason for making the hole slightly larger is that you have loosened a little soil on the bottom and around the sides of the plant, so this will help the new roots move out and find water and nutrients easily in their first couple of years. After the first couple of years, the roots will be stronger and will be able to break through the more compacted soil further out. Place the pot with the plant still inside into the hole and adjust the soil level to have it sit flush with the level of the border soil. Take the plant out of the pot; if the roots are tightly wound around, then tease them out gently. Backfill the soil around the rootball, gently firming in with your hands. You can now give the plant a good soak from a watering can. If you have some mulch then place this around the plant, but don't put it right up to the plant crown or stem, just keep it shy of this area. If you have planted in the late spring or summer, make sure that it doesn't dry out by checking regularly and watering if necessary. By year two, the plant will be able to source water lower down and you should be able to stop regular watering.

Trees are treated pretty much in the same way other than the hole you dig should be square and not round. This will make it easier for the roots to go outwards rather than in a circle. If the roots only grew in a circle, the tree would find it hard to put out stabilising roots and source water. You can also use this method with shrubs, as they are larger and also need a good root structure to stabilise them. To help find the right height to plant a tree, you can use a cane to place it over the rootball and across the planting hole. If it is level and sits on the ground then the tree has been planted to the correct level. Trees should be staked for their first two years – this stops the tree from rocking in the winds and allows the stabilising roots to develop. Here is an insider tip if you don't have any tree ties and dividers: you can use an old pair of tights or a length of hessian material as a tree tie. These are very good ties as they are very gentle on the stem of the tree and have a little bit of give in them. Remember to form a figure of eight with them so that you have that gap between the stake and the tree. Whilst the trees are establishing themselves and producing the roots that will hold them steady, staking will make sure that strong winds will not cause the tree to rock and loosen the new roots. Stakes should be removed after two years, by which time the tree will have a strong root system. Some gardeners do not stake very small trees, but as I get some very high winds in winter, I always stake mine.

▨ Lifting and dividing bulbs

As with perennials, bulbs can become congested over time and this affects their flowering. Or you may have planted them in exactly the perfect place that your new shrub will be planted. Whatever the reason, wait a few weeks after flowering has ended and the leaves start to wilt before you lift and divide them.

Bulbs which can be lifted and divided

- ➤ Crocus
- ➤ Snowdrops
- ➤ Daffodils
- ➤ Grape hyacinth
- ➤ Winter aconites
- ➤ Bluebell
- ➤ Cyclamen

I will come clean here and state that I don't have bulbs planted in my borders as I find it hard to remember where they are once the leaves die back. And then in the summer I spot a space for a new plant, dig a hole and find it is a space because there are spring bulbs there! So instead, I plant my bulbs in pots and have them placed around the garden. I also have bulbs in pots that I will place amongst the plants in the borders, taking them away when they die back. I also have bulbs planted into my lawns which give a lovely display over spring and summer. However, that is not to deny that bulbs in a border add lovely colour and movement, and if you have bulbs in the border, then here is how to divide up and replant them.

Equipment

- Spade
- Watering can with rose
- Compost or mulch

Method

Use your spade to loosen the soil around and under the clump of bulbs you want to divide, then gently lever the bulbs out of the ground. Be careful not to damage the bulbs themselves. Remove the excess soil and if you want smaller clumps, gently tease the bulbs apart. Take the bulbs to where you want them to continue growing and dig a hole which is slightly wider than what you need and also a little deeper. Make sure that you are planting them the correct way up – don't laugh, this does happen! Although, it should be easier with bulbs in the green as you have the leaves to guide you to which way is up! Bulbs are generally planted at a depth of three times their size. I use this as a general rule, although you can check for individual depths if you want a precise figure. Once in, firm the soil around the bulbs and water in well with a watering can. Add a layer of mulch over the bulbs.

Collecting seeds and how to store them

We looked at growing flowering plants from seed, that is half-hardy annuals, hardy annuals and perennials, in Chapter 5. Here I will look in more detail at how to collect and store your seeds.

As with the other propagation methods I have looked at in this chapter, collecting seed is another method you can use which will help cut costs and if you have a particular favourite plant, then you can grow more for your garden. I very much enjoy curating pots to give as gifts to friends and family. This is a good way of making a lovely floral display for the price of a new pot and some compost. I bought a packet of hardy annual poppy seeds last year, sowed them directly into some pots and they were a gorgeous pale yellow colour. They flowered for months and I wanted to grow them again this year, so I collected the seed heads in the autumn and have stored them ready to be sown in the spring. Collecting seed is also a good form of succession planning for some of your more tender plants if you are worried that harsh winter may affect them – you can store the seed heads as an insurance policy in case the parent plant does suffer through bad weather.

You should be aware that most plants we buy today are hybrid plants (also referred to as F1 plants); this means that they are grown from propagated plants. Two or more plants have been cross-pollinated to produce the plant you see growing in your garden. Why do this? Well, the growers can take a plant with vigour and resilience and cross-pollinate it with another that has beautiful flowers or in the case of vegetables, bountiful harvests. This happens with certain varieties of Aquilegia and Hellebore. But if you don't mind getting a new plant with a slightly different colour of flower, then start collecting seeds.

So, what type of plants can you collect seed from?

- Perennials
- Biennials
- Trees
- Shrubs
- Annuals
- Grasses
- Vegetables
- Herbs

So, let's get on and look at how to collect your seeds. Firstly, you will need the following:

Equipment

- Secateurs
- Brown paper bags or envelopes
- A tray or plate for drying the seeds
- A pen and a label

Method

Always collect seeds on a dry day. Wet or damp seeds will only attract mould and disease. Seeds have ripened when the casing covering them has gone from green to brown. Seeds develop around one to two months after flowering has taken place. So, it is important to keep a regular check on your seed heads as they may be ready to collect quite suddenly.

Seeds that are contained in a hard outer casing are collected by removing the stalk from the plant using your secateurs, keeping the seed head intact. You can put these on a plate or a tray to dry. This can be in a greenhouse or a covered cold frame if you have one, or on a windowsill. Leave until the seed head is completely dry and you can then remove the seeds.

You might be familiar with the term, removing the wheat from the chaff. Well, you might find that you have some of the outer casing mixed in with your seeds and it is important to remove this. This is to avoid the chaff rotting and affecting the health of your seeds. One way of doing this is to put the seeds in your cupped hand and gently blow on the seeds; any chaff will be removed and the heavier seeds will remain in your hand.

Some seed heads are called achene or as most people refer to them fluffy seed heads – these are seen on a clematis, for example. To collect these, just grab the seed head and pull the seeds off in your hand. Put these into a paper bag or envelope.

There are seed heads which explode and distribute their seeds this way, such as the poppy. Carefully take the seed head in your hand and bend the stem over so that the seeds can fall into your paper bag or envelope.

The seeds from berries are collected when the fruit is still ripe. You can try this with redcurrants, blackcurrants and blueberries. Remove the berries and crush them gently on a plate, then carefully remove the seeds. You can use the end of a pencil or something similar to do this. Lay the seeds on a piece of kitchen roll and leave them to dry. Once they have dried, you can store them in a paper bag or envelope.

Your collected seeds must be stored in a cool and dry environment, such as a garage or cool area of the house.

I store my seeds in a wooden box which is kept in a cool area of the house. Don't be tempted to leave them in your greenhouse or shed as they may well get damp in the winter and your seeds will more than likely be mouldy when you come to look at them next spring.

I use paper bags or old paper envelopes to store my seeds. Always remember to write on your paper bag/envelope which seeds are in there and which year they were collected! I know, you think you will remember what is in there, but believe me, you won't! If kept in the correct environment, your seeds should be viable for several years.

Top 7 key points when propagating plants

1. Softwood cuttings are taken in the summer months from the fresh new growth of the current year. Take these cuttings in the morning.

2. Hardwood cuttings are taken in the autumn and winter; the growth will be less flexible than the softwood cuttings.

3. Propagation by layering is best carried out in the spring or autumn. This method works for both deciduous and evergreen shrubs.

4. Lifting and dividing perennials is a cost-effective way of increasing your stock of plants and can be carried out at any time of the year. Spring and autumn are preferable as the plants will be dormant.

5. If buying established plants from a nursery or garden centre, always remember to check the health of the plant before you buy it. Look for lush growth, no breakages to stems and a good root system.

6. Check the return policy if you are buying plants online as you won't see the plant until it arrives at your door.

7. Collect seeds on a dry day, and remove the chaff. Only store seeds that are completely dry, placing them in a paper bag or envelope. Remember to label your seeds and keep them in a cool and dry environment.

Are you now going to try out each of these methods for propagating your plants? I do hope so – it is cost-effective and very satisfying. But once your plants are in the ground and established, how do you keep them looking their best and as healthy as they were when you planted them? That is what we are about to look at in the next chapter.

Notes

_____

_____

_____

_____

_____

_____

_____

_____

_____

_____

_____

_____

_____

_____

_____

_____

_____

_____

Chapter Seven

A Guide to Pruning

"A garden requires patient labour and attention. Plants do not grow merely to satisfy ambitions or to fulfil good intentions. They thrive because someone expended effort on them."

Liberty Hyde Bailey

"All gardening is landscape painting."

William Kent

I enjoy pruning, I find it a very satisfying and mindful activity. There is a very satisfying rhythm to pruning. Pruning gives you another opportunity to be immersed in your garden and at the same time you can check on the health of the plants in the garden whilst you prune. Pruning can be quite daunting at first – so many rules and guidelines! But once you understand the basic rules, prune at the right time and back to the right place, then you are on the road to successful pruning. In Chapter 1 we looked at garden tools and the jobs they do. We will now look in more detail at some of those garden tools as they will be very useful now that we are tackling pruning. Together we will demystify the dark art of pruning.

▨ Why do we prune?

There are several reasons for carrying out pruning of your plants, I have listed them below.

- ➤ Encourage new growth
- ➤ Control the size of the plant
- ➤ Improve the overall shape
- ➤ Maintain and improve the health of your plants
- ➤ Maximise fruit production
- ➤ Promote the growth of flowers

Let's take each of these points and look at them in more detail.

Encourage new growth

The stems of the Cornus are cut down each spring which stimulates the growth of fresh new stems that provide the vibrant winter colour that we enjoy. In woody shrubs such as the Philadelphus or Weigela, cutting down every second or third of the older stems each year (after they have finished flowering) opens up the structure of the plant, giving it better air circulation and it will encourage new young stems to grow, which will provide you with a good show of flowers next year.

Control the size of the plant

If you leave some shrubs without pruning them, they will very soon outgrow the area that they inhabit and may have a detrimental effect on the other plants and shrubs nearby. The Buddleia, Sambucus and Forsythia are two very good examples of this. You may also want to keep plants to a more manageable height, or to a height that doesn't cause shadow or annoy the neighbours!

Improve the overall shape

If you prune young plants, you are helping to create the shape they will have as mature plants. Hedges are pruned to keep their shape as well as examples of topiary in some gardens. Lavender is pruned yearly to help maintain its compact shape and avoid it becoming unruly and leggy.

Maintain and improve the health of your plants

My pruning mantra is to follow the 3 Ds – that is, remove dead, diseased and dying stems and then look for crossing stems and deal with these. Crossing stems will rub and cause damage to the bark of the stem which can in turn lead to disease.

Maximise fruit production

It is really important to prune fruit trees in winter and then again in the summer to maximise the flowering and ultimately the fruit production of the tree. Shrub fruits such as redcurrant and blackcurrant need to be pruned to keep an open shape which allows for good ventilation, and this will also help with consistent fruit production. Cane fruits such as raspberries are cut down to encourage new fresh canes to grow.

Promote the growth of flowers

The purpose of a flowering plant is to produce flowers which will in turn produce seed that will create the next generation. To prolong the flowering season of a perennial or annual, it is important to remove the spent flowers, which will encourage the plant to produce new flowers. For flowering shrubs, it is important to remove the old spent flowers to enable the plant to produce new and hopefully higher numbers of flowers in the next growing season.

When to prune

Prune spring and early summer flowering shrubs as soon as they have stopped flowering – these include Forsythia, Philadelphus, Weigela, Kerria and Lilac. The flowers of these shrubs are carried on growth that has been produced the year before flowering happens. Prune at the end of spring, then the plant will put on new growth over the coming months and it is from this growth that the flowers will grow the following spring. If left too late in the season, then the plant may not have time to produce any new growth before the winter and will result in reduced flowering or even no flowering at all.

Evergreen shrubs should not be pruned until late spring or early summer and not in autumn or winter months. Prune after flowering, or for non-flowering evergreen shrubs, then wait until the last frost has passed.

Shrubs that flower from July to October should be pruned in spring as they will produce flowers on new growth produced in the current year. Examples of these are Buddleia, Sambucus, Hydrangea paniculata and Fuchsia.

You can prune fruit trees in winter and again in summer. Pruning in winter will promote new growth to be produced, and pruning in the summer is to cut back excess growth and channel energy to the fruit. For example, you can prune your apple trees in early summer to remove any leggy soft growth as this growth is taking energy from the growing fruit. In winter, this is when you prune to shape the tree and tackle dead, diseased, dying and crossing stems.

Many evergreen shrubs don't need regular pruning, other than to remove spent flowers. Pruning is carried out if the plant needs to be shaped or to control its size. Pruning can affect flowering in some cases, such as rhododendron and camellia. But if they have to be pruned and some flowering is impacted the year after, you will know that the flowering the year after that will be back to normal.

▨ Tools to use when pruning

- ➢ Secateurs
- ➢ Loppers
- ➢ Long-handled or extending loppers
- ➢ Hand saw
- ➢ Hand shears
- ➢ Hedge cutter (battery, electric or petrol)

- ➤ Chainsaw (battery or petrol)
- ➤ Topiary shears

Bypass and anvil secateurs will easily cut fresh stems of up to 1.5cm easily and cleanly. The bypass secateurs will also cut slightly thicker stems and stems which are old wood. The key to successful pruning is that the blades are very sharp and clean. Make a positive cut, and if you feel that you are having to strain to cut then you need a different tool, a lopper probably.

Loppers can also have bypass or anvil blades and the same applies to what they can tackle. They will both cut stems bigger than your secateurs can manage and the bypass loppers will be able to cut larger stems than the anvil type.

Long-handled or extending loppers are useful if you need to prune branches or stems that you can't reach with your loppers. Using these means that you can cut branches up to around three metres from the ground without having to stand on a ladder.

A hand saw will be your tool of choice if the stem is too big for your loppers or is dead wood. Most hand saws work by cutting on the pull movement. That is, when you pull the blade towards you. So, use pressure on the pull movement and you will get a nice clean cut. Here's a tip: if you are removing a branch or heavy stem then cut off some of the weight of the branch before you make the final cut at the trunk or base of the shrub. If the branch is heavy and falls, you risk a tear at the cut which could mean that disease could enter at the wound. Take some of the weight off before you make the final cut, and you can avoid this.

Hand shears are very useful for light shaping of shrubs or taking light growth off a hedge. They are also useful for any topiary you might be carrying out. They can be used to cut back the old flowering stems of lavender.

Hedge cutters, as the name suggests, are for cutting and shaping hedges. They will cut through new growth easily and older stems of around 1.5cm. Remember to wear eye and ear protection when using these machines and be aware of those around you who might move into your path.

Chainsaws can be used to cut trunks or very large stems and will make light work of this. However, they are a specialist tool and it is probably best to either get training and protective gear, or leave it to an expert to use these.

Topiary shears are used for the finer trimming of shaped shrubs and hedges. When you need precision cuts.

Always use the correct tool for the type of pruning you are carrying out, and make sure that it is clean and that the blades are sharp.

How to prune

Always cut back to something, whether it is a leaf bud, a flower bud, above a leaf joint or the end of a stem. Make your cut clean and around 1 cm from the bud and sloping in the same direction as the bud. If you are cutting above two buds on either side of the stem – see the next photograph – then the cut should be straight across. How do you tell the difference between a flower bud and a leaf bud? Generally speaking, a leaf bud is small and pointed. A flower bud tends to be rounder in shape and plumper.

Making a cut above two new leaf buds

Shrubs

Remember the mantra: cut back dead, diseased, dying and crossing stems. I always start any pruning project by removing any stems that fall into these categories. This may be all you have to do at this point, but it will help maintain the health and shape of your plants. You can then look to maintain good airflow by pruning to get an open shape. This can involve cutting some older stems down to the ground or pruning to an outward-facing bud – by doing this you are encouraging the new growth to grow outwards rather than into the plant. You can also cut out any weak shoots as they will take essential energy from the healthier shoots. With pruning, it is always a good idea to take your time, stand back and check the shape before you cut any more, then you can go back in and do more pruning. I have lifted the crown or raised the canopy of a couple of my shrubs by pruning the growth of the stems from the ground up to the height I want the canopy to begin. This exposes the stems which become a feature within the garden; it also allows light underneath the shrub and allows me to plant around the base of the shrub. It is also useful if the shrub is beside a path as it will make it easier to pass by if the canopy is above head height. See the next photo for an example of crown lifting I have carried out on my Photinia Red Robin.

Crown lifted Photinia Red Robin

Climbers

If you have wall or fence trained plants such as a climbing rose, then you should choose a bud pointing inwards towards the wall or fence. My climbing rose is attached to the fence with three rows of wires. I have established six stems. Each of these stems is trained along the wires horizontally. You should aim for a strong structure like this, as it is much easier to maintain and you get good flowering as the structure is open and all of the plants can get maximum exposure to the sun. I cut each of the growing stems back to the last bud each autumn, and in the spring the growth comes from this point with flower buds forming. If any rogue stems grow outwards, I just cut these back to the main stem.

Fruit trees

Fruit trees need good airflow, so you need to prune these to have an open centre and no crossing branches. Imagine the shape of a goblet – this is what you are aiming for. In the late autumn or early winter, before the frosts, I will cut the new growth back to a spur (the spur is where the flower bud will grow from and eventually produce the fruit). I also cut out any diseased, dying or crossing stems. If you miss the cut in autumn, you can also do this right up to the end of February or March, depending on where you live. You just need to avoid frosty days or when frost is forecast overnight.

The open, goblet shape also applies to currants, blueberries and Lonicera kamtschatica. To create this shape, you should remove every 2nd or 3rd of the oldest stems, cutting them right down to the ground. You should reduce the overall height and width by taking the stems back by three or four leaf nodes.

Grasses

Deciduous grasses should be cut down to the ground when you see the new shoots appear in spring, but remember to be careful not to cut the new growth emerging from the soil. Evergreen grasses should not be cut; instead, in spring put a pair of gloves on and pull your fingers through the grass, the old stems and seed heads will come away from the plant.

Perennials

The old flower heads of perennials should be cut back regularly as this will encourage new flowers to appear. Towards autumn you should leave the flowers to go to seed and leave these standing over the winter. This is great for birds who will feed on the seeds, and insects who can shelter amongst the stems. The green growth of the perennial will turn brown over winter; again, don't prune this back until spring when you see the new growth coming through the ground. By leaving this old growth on over winter, you are creating a habitat for insects to shelter over the colder months.

Hedges

Hedges are pruned, generally speaking, once or twice a year. This depends on the type of hedge you have, of course, and how well clipped you like it to be. Always remember that you shouldn't prune hedges during nesting season for birds. So, before you start, check when this is relevant for your area – and I always stand back, listening for any noises from nests; watch for a while and you will see if the adult birds are going back and forth to a nest. Failing that, have a careful look in the hedge. If your hedge is starting to block a path or entranceway and it's the nesting season or there is a nest in there, you can very carefully take a pair of hand shears and clip the overhanging stems from the path. The actual hedge cut will have to wait until the chicks have left the nest.

Shrub roses

Shrub roses should be pruned in the late autumn to reduce their height. This prevents wind rock during any winter winds which can damage their roots. Prune to an outward-facing bud at around half their height. At the same time, remove any dead, diseased, dying or crossing stems. It is also worth pruning out any weak stems to the ground at this point. In the spring, you can then prune again, taking the height down by about a third, and prune to an outward bud to maintain an open, well-ventilated shape.

Cane fruit

When it comes to how to prune cane fruit such as raspberries, there are two methods based on the type of raspberry you have. Summer fruiting raspberries will fruit on growth put on in the previous year, so don't prune these new shoots. Instead, prune down to the ground the shoots that carried this year's fruit. Tie in the new shoots to your support structure. Autumn fruiting raspberries produce fruit on the current year's growth – that is the growth it will put on next spring. So, in autumn you cut down all the shoots. In spring, the new shoots will appear and you can tie these in as they get bigger.

After pruning

After pruning, give your plants, shrubs and trees a good soak with rainwater and then apply a good layer of mulch around them. This will help the plant to recover quickly from the loss of stems. Depending on how much has been pruned, it can be quite a shock for the plant, so a good drink and feed is welcomed.

Top 7 things to remember about pruning

1. Always use the correct tool for the specific type of pruning you are carrying out. Make sure that the blades are sharp and clean.

2. Prune dead, diseased and dying stems as soon as you see them. Also, be aware of crossing stems and remove them when spotted.

3. Prune at the correct time of year or you risk losing flower or fruit growth. If in doubt, refer back to the start of this chapter or consult the RHS website for information.

4. Always prune back to something: a leaf bud, flower bud or the end of a stem.

5. Check hedges for nesting birds before you start cutting them.

6. Regular deadheading of perennials and annuals will promote more flower growth.

7. Take your time when pruning, stand back and check the shape, look to see where any more pruning is needed. You can always go back and prune some more, but you can't put the cut stems back on the plant!

So, that's all about pruning. This chapter aimed to give you some of the basic tools to start pruning with confidence and I hope that it has achieved that. Like anything new, start with easier deadheading, get your confidence and move on to the more complex pruning. I think the best tip is to study your plants, see how they grow, where they grow from, what shape you want them, and how would you prune to make that shape. If you are not sure, ask someone or look up helpful resources online. Oh, and remember to prune at the right time of year!

Notes

_____

_____

_____

_____

_____

_____

_____

_____

_____

_____

_____

_____

_____

_____

_____

_____

_____

_____

Chapter Eight

Using What Nature Gives Us and Repurposing Items

"One touch of nature makes the whole world kin."

William Shakespeare

"The biggest obstacle to good gardening is the desire to know the answer and not the questions."

Monty Don

What do plants need to live and thrive? The right growing conditions, healthy soil and access to water. In Chapter 5 we looked at choosing plants that are suited to your garden's particular climate and environment. And in Chapter 2 we looked at the importance of having healthy soil so that your plants will continue to thrive. I have touched on the subject of when and how to water your plants throughout the previous chapters. In this chapter, I will take you through some ways you can meet all these needs, not by buying in products, but by producing your own using what nature already provides us with.

I know that some of what we are about to discuss may not be possible to do in your own garden space, but it is useful to know, and you never know, you might find a suitable spot to put some or all of these methods into use.

▨ Comfrey tea

I feed my fruit, vegetables and pots with a comfrey tea that I make myself and today was the day when I decanted the, to be truthful, obnoxious-smelling comfrey tea. I grow my comfrey plants in the garden to harvest the leaves from. It can be quite invasive, so grow in an area where if it spreads it doesn't take over your borders. Or grow in a pot that you sink into the ground and that should stop the plant from colonising the border. Comfrey takes huge quantities of nutrients from deep in the soil and stores them in its leaves. Comfrey has high levels of nitrogen, phosphorus and potassium, and feeding your plants and vegetables with this potent mix will help flower and fruit production. When you harvest the leaves, let them break down and you end up with a rich, dark and nutrient-rich feed. As it is high in potassium, this is excellent for feeding flowering plants and fruits including tomatoes. You can also take the leaves off and put them straight down around the base of your plants; roses especially love this. As the leaves break down, they will release the beneficial nutrients. You can also add the leaves directly into pots and cover them with your compost. If you would like to benefit from the power of comfrey, then let's make some tea...

To make your comfrey tea you will need:

Equipment

- Comfrey leaves, chopped up into small pieces
- A large tub with a lid – I use an old tub that once held granular feed. You must have a lid to keep the smell in!
- A large stone or brick – I use an old terracotta pot
- Water
- Bottles to decant the feed into
- A corner of the garden to let it sit and mature

Method

Fill your tub or bucket with the chopped-up leaves, right to the top and then place your brick or stone on top of the leaves. This will weigh them down and help the breakdown process. Then fill the tub with water to the top. Seal up the tub and place it in a quiet corner of the garden. I say a quiet corner, but it is best to have it stored away from the day-to-day areas, in case you can smell the tub and its contents! I leave it for about four weeks to allow the leaves to break down fully. You can leave it longer if you want. I decant the liquid into old juice bottles and store them in the shed. But you can leave the liquid in the tub and just take out the amount you need each time. But I prefer to have the feed in bottles, it is just easier to handle and I can use the tub again to make more tea. Once I have taken all the liquid out, just the leaves remain and I put this in my compost heap. Absolutely nothing is wasted. When you next have access to a good supply of comfrey leaves, start the process over again.

To use your lovely feed, add it to your watering can at a rate of one part comfrey feed to ten litres of water. You can also use this liquid as a foliar feed. Use the same dilution amounts and add to a sprayer or mister and spray it onto the leaves of your plants.

I use a watering can and feed my pots that contain plants such as roses, Lonicera (the edible variety), wallflowers, bulbs and strawberries. The raspberries and blueberries prefer acidic soil, so I also use an ericaceous feed (I do not make this myself though). I also use the comfrey feed on my fruit and vegetables growing in the borders and raised beds. These include tomatoes, redcurrants, courgettes, dwarf French beans and peas.

Comfrey tea ready to be decanted into bottles

Bottles filled with comfrey tea mixture

Seaweed feed

You can use the same method to make a rich seaweed feed yourself. A seaweed feed is great for your fruits and vegetables and can help prevent blossom end rot that often occurs on tomato plants. But check first whether you are allowed to collect seaweed from your local beach.

Nettle feed

Another great free feed that you can make is by using nettles to make a liquid feed for your plants. Nettles have very high levels of chlorophyll, nitrogen, iron and potassium, which will encourage leaf growth and feed hungry plants such as your annuals, perennials, shrubs and fruit trees. Use the same method as described above to make your nettle tea.

▨ Water

We all have to be very aware of our water usage and, if we do have to water our gardens, make sure that we do this efficiently. First and foremost, collect rainwater.

A water butt is a must, if you have the space for one. I have a 100-litre slimline water butt which is tucked away and is connected to a drainpipe at the side of the house. I also plan to install guttering and a down pipe on my shed to collect water in a second water butt. When rain is forecast, I also put out all of my buckets and trugs to collect water. I have bought a large cattle trough to collect water in – it can store up to 400 litres of water. Just in case any creature is unfortunate enough to fall in the trough, buckets or pond, I tie a length of netting to the handles and let it trail in the water. This acts as a stepladder to help creatures crawl out.

It is amazing to see just how much water you can collect. Plants much prefer rainwater, but if you have to use tap water you should fill your watering can or buckets and let it sit for around 24 hours to allow for any chemicals in the tap water to dissipate. Please do not use a sprinkler to water your garden – it doesn't do an effective job of watering plants and is so wasteful. Much better to use a watering can.

To make sure you water effectively and with as little water as possible, always water at the very base of the plant – the water will get straight to the roots. Do this in the morning or later in the day when the sun isn't so strong. This will avoid evaporation and make sure that you use the water most effectively.

Limiting the amount of exposed soil is also a good way of reducing the need to water your plants. Another very good excuse to buy or grow more plants in your garden! Mulching the ground around your plants will help stop the evaporation of water from the surface of the soil. We looked at mulch in Chapter 1 and I explained that the term mulch refers to anything covering exposed soil. This could be compost, soil conditioner, bark, cardboard, leaf mould or grass clippings. Remember to moisten the soil before you put a mulch down – you are looking to seal in moisture and if the soil is dry when you do this, you will only be sealing in parched soil.

Pots will dry out very quickly as the plants in them have no access to water deeper down in the ground. I always cover the top of the soil in pots with grit as this will reduce the rate of evaporation and therefore the need to water so often. You can also move your pots out of direct sunshine, and this will reduce the need for watering.

If you have new plants in the garden beds then you may have to water them during dry spells as they won't have developed a good root system which will seek out water deeper down in the soil. I would do this for their first year in the ground and after that they should be able to cope on their own. Keep an eye on very large evergreen shrubs – if they are distressed, they will start to drop their leaves. They can afford to lose some of their leaves, but if they lose the majority, you may lose the shrub. The same goes for evergreen trees.

If you are growing vegetables, you can take some precautions to reduce the amount of watering you will need to carry out. These are very similar to what I have discussed in the previous paragraphs. And, if you grow in raised beds, then the plants may struggle to access water from the ground, so in this instance, you may have to water. So, mulch around your vegetables/fruit. Water, only if necessary, and water directly at the roots. I have found that by interplanting with flowers such as Calendula, Nasturtium, Echium and Borage, these plants cover the ground around the vegetables and help to reduce water loss through evaporation. We will be looking more closely at companion planting in Chapter 9.

This may be a controversial point of view, but I wouldn't water your lawn at all. Grass is very tough and will recover very quickly when the next rainfall comes. The only time you should water your lawn is when it is first laid and you need the roots to establish, or if you have re-seeded areas of your lawn. Once the lawn is established, it really can look after itself. I know it looks worrying when the grass starts to brown, but we all know, the rain will come!

Here are two very effective homemade drip water systems you might like to try out.

The first is to take an old juice bottle, cut the bottom off the bottle and remove the cap. Insert the bottle top first into the ground near the plant you need to water or in a pot – this is especially good for watering pots – fill with your collected rainwater and this will gently release water into the surrounding soil.

Making your own Olla to water your plants is a very simple and extremely efficient way to keep your plants hydrated. This method of watering plants has been around for centuries, so has a very good proven record! You should remove the Olla before the winter frosts as the terracotta pots may break. When the spring comes you can put them out into the soil again.

How to make your own Olla

Equipment

- One terracotta pot
- Silicone sealant
- Terracotta or plastic water tray
- A stone or brick
- Watering can

Method

Seal the hole at the bottom of your terracotta pot using silicone sealant or something similar. Then bury the pot in the soil near to the plants you wish to water, I use this method when I grow my tomato plants. Fill the pot with the rainwater you have collected and cover the top of the pot with a water tray or similar. To reduce the likelihood of the tray blowing away in strong winds, you can weigh this down with a large stone or brick. As the terracotta is porous, water will slowly leach out of the pot and into the surrounding soil. Ingenious! Just remember to top it up when water levels get low.

Making olla pots

Olla pots inserted into the ground

Grey water – not a very enticing term, is it? But this is a way of watering our plants in the short term and during prolonged dry weather. So, what do we mean by grey water? You can use water from your shower, a bath or the kitchen sink to water your plants. The soil or potting compost will be pretty effective in filtering out any residual soap detergent in the water. But this method must only be used in the short term as continued use will put a strain on the soil/compost and it won't be able to filter out the residues in the water. Water collected from these sources shouldn't be used on any of your edibles though. For them, you can use the water from cooking your vegetables. Any water using this method must be used within 24 hours to avoid any possible bacterial growth.

Finally, with the changes to our climate, we should all be looking at growing plants that will be suitable to the climate as it is now and how it looks likely to become in the future. Certainly, here in the UK, the summer temperatures are rising and we have had some quite prolonged periods without rain. The reservoirs are filled during the winter, so we rely on sufficient rainfall over winter to provide us with water in the summer months.

So, with a bit of thought, careful watering and water collection, we can all reduce our water consumption.

▨ Compost and leaf mould

By far and away the best thing you can do for your garden's health and vigour is to make your own compost and leaf mould. Not only does it save you money, it also improves your soil health and helps to retain moisture in your soil.

If you make your compost using your garden waste, you are taking the nutrients and bacterial activity from your garden and then this is replicated in your compost which you will then add back into your garden. The same goes for collecting fallen leaves from your garden and making leaf mould. An extremely good example of the circular economy and zero waste! As well as saving you a lot of money on buying compost or mulch, of course.

I do appreciate that some of you reading this have smaller gardens and to make your compost or leaf mould will require some space, but if you can make room to do this then it will be worth it. Let's look in a little more detail about how to create your own compost and leaf mould.

So, what exactly is compost? It is a mix of organic material added to a heap which will be broken down by bacterial, insect and worm activity. The fungi-like bacteria which aids the breakdown of the more woody type materials is called actinomycetes. When you add your organic material to your compost heap then the bacteria gets to work breaking down the material; this in turn increases the temperature of the heap, which also aids the breakdown of your material. Then the worms and insects get to work and break everything down even further. You will find slugs, spiders, centipedes, worms and ground beetles among the animals which will reside in your compost heap. To further help speed up the process, it is important that whatever you put on your heap is as small as you can make it, so that means shredding any cardboard and chopping up any vegetation. Your compost heap should never smell – if it does, it means that there is too much nitrogen-rich material. You need the correct mix of nitrogen and carbon. The optimal mix of nitrogen and carbon should roughly be 30 parts carbon to one part nitrogen.

Simply put, nitrogen materials are anything green such as grass, kitchen waste or new stems from pruning, whereas carbon is found in dead stems or cardboard. I have listed below what you can put on your compost heap – this is a guide to get you started and is not exhaustive. I have marked the nitrogen items with an N and carbon with a C.

Compost bays covered with old hessian backed carpet.

Compost bays showing new bay on right and turned compost in the left bay

What can be added to a compost heap?

- Uncooked kitchen waste such as peelings, eggshells, tea bags (unbleached and containing no glued seams), spoilt vegetables and fruit (N)
- Any green stems or plant material from pruning or home-grown vegetable plants after harvesting (N)
- Dead stems from pruning – these should be shredded or cut into small pieces before going on the heap (C)
- Older stems from pruning – again these should be shredded or cut into small pieces before going on the heap (N)
- Grass clippings – I only put grass clippings that don't contain any seed heads or weed seed heads (N)
- Shredded cardboard from packaging, making sure there are no labels or packing tape attached (C)
- Inner cardboard tubes from toilet paper or kitchen rolls (C)
- Shredded paper (C)
- Seaweed (N)

- Comfrey or nettle leaves (N)
- Feathers or animal and human hair (C)
- Used compost from pots that have had annuals grown in them (C)

What shouldn't be put on a compost heap

- Meat or fish, cooked or raw – this will attract vermin
- Cat litter tray materials
- Weed seed heads
- Cooked bones

Home composting methods will not get to a high enough temperature to kill any weed seeds or indeed seed heads from your plants, so it is always best to keep from putting these on your heap as they may germinate when you come to use your compost around the garden.

There are several ways to reduce the size of the material you put on the heap, you can use secateurs or loppers to chop them up, or you can use a garden shredder – this is particularly good for reducing the size of stems. I have an electric shredder and it means that stems that I would normally put in the garden waste bin can now be shredded and added to the compost heap. If I am putting cardboard or brown paper on the compost, then I just tear the pieces up by hand.

I have made my compost bays using wooden boards and chicken wire. So, the sides of the bays are made up of wooden boards, which are secured at the corners with posts. The chicken wire divides the bays and is at the front of the bays. A compost heap needs to have air circulating it. This will provide the heap with oxygen as the microorganisms in the compost heap need oxygen. And it is also important to allow the decomposition gases to escape. You can buy plastic compost bins, but I found that because there was no air circulation, the decomposition just didn't work as effectively. Do your research if you are going to use a plastic compost bin and find one that does have vents to allow for air circulation.

The other important factor is to keep the compost heap moist as this aids decomposition, so if the weather has been particularly dry, you may have to soak the heap. I use an old piece of hessian-backed carpet to cover my compost heap as this lets in moisture but will also keep the heat in.

You can also buy or make compost bays from slatted wood; these are good for all the reasons stated above. Make sure that you can remove the front pieces of wood as you will need access to either turn or remove your composted materials. The chicken wire on the front of my bays can be rolled back to allow me access.

The ideal set-up for your compost heaps is to have three bays. The first bay is for the current heap, so the materials you are adding this year. The second bay is for bay one to be turned in at the end of the year. Then, bay two is put into bay three and this is the compost bay that you will use for your supply of compost. I move my compost in September each year. I prefer to do this at this time because we have frogs that like to hang out in the compost heap and if I leave this job for the winter then I would disturb them when they are settling in for the winter months. So, from September to the following September, I use bay one to add my materials. Then I move the heap from bay two to bay three. Now bay three will be the compost I use in the garden over the coming year. I move bay one to bay two and start a new heap in bay one. Each of the bays will be covered in a carpet. When I move bay one to bay two, I have to rummage around and temporarily move the frogs into a bucket; once the job is complete, I put the frogs back into bay two and they will make their way back to bay one once there is enough new material in there.

We looked at the mix of carbon and nitrogen that you add to your compost heap. I manage this by layering what I put in there. So, if there is a good layer of nitrogen-rich materials, i.e. kitchen scraps and fresh cuttings, then I will add a good thick layer of carbon-rich materials such as shredded paper and cardboard. To speed up the process of decomposition, you should ideally turn your compost regularly using a garden fork. This gets everything mixed up and allows some air into the heap. But I don't turn my compost because of the frogs! I don't want to put a fork into the heap as I know that they are in there. This lack of turning hasn't had much of an impact on the rate at which my heap breaks down. Nevertheless, I would say, the best practice is to turn it, but if you can't, just make sure that you layer your mix of materials well and make sure that what you put in there is broken into as small pieces as you can get them. Finally, if you don't have room for three bays then two will do – you can substitute bay three with old compost bags which you can fill with your ready-to-use compost and store somewhere dry until you need to use them.

Your lovely homemade compost can be used as a mulch around your garden beds and added to potting compost for your pots. I also use my compost to add to my raised vegetable beds each year. This helps to replace lost nutrients from the vegetables that were grown in the beds in the previous year. This means that I don't have to use any granular feed on the beds.

Another great way to use what your garden gives you is to make your leaf mould, but what exactly is leaf mould and how would you use it? Leaf mould is produced when the leaves that fall in autumn are broken down by fungi and produce a lovely crumbly mix which you can use to mulch borders or add to your potting compost. Now, you can let your fallen leaves lie on your borders and they will break down over time and add to your hummus layer – nature will mulch your borders for you! I do this; I only remove leaves from the lawns, paths and any that land on the plants. The leaves that you do collect can be gathered together and either be added to a leaf bay (similar to the compost bays) and left until the next autumn to be used, or you can collect them and put them into old compost or bin bags. If you use the bag method, remember to puncture some holes into the bags and give the leaves a soak before tying the bags up. You can then store the bags in a corner of the garden and within a year you will have lovely friable leaf mould. If you have room to have a bay, then this should be soaked and covered. To speed up the decomposition process, you can collect your leaves and lay them on your lawn, raise the height of your mower blades and mow the leaves. They will be in very small pieces now and you can add to your bay/bags. This is good as the leaves will now break down much quicker. Leaf mould is not as high in nutrients as your homemade compost, but it is still extremely useful as a mulch which adds organic matter to the surface of your soil, acts as a weed suppressant and helps to retain moisture, which in turn will cut down on your need to water in dry spells. When you add leaf mould to your potting compost, it will help to retain moisture in the pot as well as adding nutrients.

▧ Repurposing everyday items

Not strictly 'what nature gives us' – but we can make a difference to the environment and climate by repurposing items that we already have lying around. I don't know about you, but before anything is consigned to the bin or recycling, I always think 'What can I use this for?' – I just don't like waste, never have, and use everything until it is completely broken. I also like a challenge, I like to see how I can use something for a different purpose which gives it new life. And, as a result, I have many small bundles of odd items that I know one day will come in very useful! I have listed some of the items that I have stored and re-purposed to give you some ideas. You have probably some very ingenious uses for items yourselves – if so, please share your ideas.

➢ **Old compost bags** – I use these to put leaves in to produce leaf mould (see previous paragraphs) and I have used them to grow potatoes in. I was given some decorative grit that someone was going to throw out and decanted this into some old compost bags and these are now stored away ready to use when the need arises.

➢ **Bricks and cobbles** – I have used these to create paths, and weigh down the cover on my ollas and in my small pond to create different depths and a platform for the plants. You can sink bricks into your borders to create stepping stones.

➢ **Terracotta pots** – if these are chipped or cracked you can use these as bug hotels, add dry sticks and straw then leave them on their side in a quiet corner. You can also break them up and use these as crock. Crock is the term for a curved piece of broken pot which is laid over the drainage hole at the bottom of a pot to stop compost blocking the drainage hole.

➢ **If there is a hole in your metal bucket** or watering can, you can use these to plant into – just make sure you add enough additional drainage holes.

➢ **Plastic plant pots** can be used over and over again until they are broken. Some nurseries will also take them to recycle them. You can also cut the bottom off a plastic pot and use the rest as a shield around young vegetable plants, just to make it that little bit harder for snails and slugs to get to. I also use plastic pots to cover the tops of canes that are supporting my tomato plants – this stops me from getting a painful poke in the eye!

➤ **Pieces of wood** – I have quite a collection of pieces of wood! I managed to build a new raised bed with some lengths of wood I had stored. I was given a pile of batons from a friend which came with her fence panels. These come in very useful as plant supports for things such as peas and tomatoes. I use small lengths of decking boards (offcuts) to put across my raised beds so that I can stand on them instead of the soil. Odd pieces of wood can be used to make your compost or leaf mould bays.

➤ **I collect cardboard** from deliveries and use this to cover my empty vegetable beds over the winter. This keeps the weeds down and the cats off the beds. I remove any labels and sticky tape before I put the cardboard on the beds as this will not break down. In the spring

I add a layer of compost over this cardboard and plant through it (the cardboard will have broken down over the winter months so this is quite easy to do). Cardboard is also good as a weed suppressant if you are creating a new bed or have an area heavily infested with grass or perennial weeds. Put the cardboard over the area and weigh it down with your spare bricks or cobbles! Or add a layer of compost if you want to plant immediately.

➢ **Coconut shells** are also useful as crock. I use a hammer and break the shell into smaller pieces and these can be used at the bottom of your pots to stop the drainage hole from being blocked by compost.

➢ **Tights** can be used as tree ties. Tie in a figure of eight and adjust to allow for some movement. Being a soft material and flexible, this is a good method to avoid any damage to young trees.

➢ **Buckets and basins** can be put out when you know rain is coming and you can collect the rainwater.

➢ **Bubblewrap** is something that is quite difficult to recycle and you can collect quite a lot of it just from deliveries you receive. I also have a collection of bubble wrap in the shed. I use this to wrap around my pots to protect them from the frosts in winter. You can remove it in spring, store it and use it again later in the year.

➤ **As well as shredding toilet roll tubes** for adding to your compost heap, you can use these to sow your seeds into. When the seedling is big enough, you just plant the whole thing out into the garden.

➤ **Old broom handles** can be used as stakes – just remove or saw off the handle from the brush and you have yourself a stake.

➤ **Old or broken spades and forks,** you can saw off the handle, sharpen the end to a point and you can use this as a dibber.

➤ **You can provide the birds with nesting material** by collecting pieces of wool, fluff, and dog fur (from grooming), and if you de-bobble your woollen items this can be collected too. I use an old bird feeder and fill it with this material, hanging from a branch within a large shrub. You can also use some wire to tie loosely around the material, create a loop of wire at one end and hang from a branch.

Cleared raised beds covered with cardboard for
overwintering, weighted down with old bricks

Top 7 takeaways from this chapter

1. Always shred or cut into small pieces anything you put on your compost heap.

2. Make sure you have the correct proportions of carbon and nitrogen materials.

3. Keep the compost heap from drying out as this will speed up the decomposition of the materials.

4. Prioritise what needs to be watered and water efficiently. Collect as much rainwater as you can.

5. Make your fertiliser from comfrey, nettles or seaweed.

6. Before you throw anything out, see if you can find a new purpose for it around the garden.

7. Try to consume less than you produce.

I hope that this chapter gave you some good ideas about how we can garden sustainably and efficiently. I think it's in gardeners' nature to try to give more back to nature than we take. I think we are also very aware that resources are precious and anything we do, no matter how small, can make a huge difference. In the next chapter, we will look at growing your own fruit and vegetables.

Notes

_____

_____

_____

_____

_____

_____

_____

_____

_____

_____

_____

_____

_____

_____

_____

_____

_____

Chapter Nine

Growing Your Own Fruit And Vegetables

"It is only the farmer who faithfully plants seeds in the Spring, who reaps a harvest in the Autumn."

B. C. Forbes

"There is nothing that is comparable to it, as satisfactory or as thrilling as gathering vegetables one has grown."

Alice B. Toklas

I love my garden and get so much pleasure from planning how it looks, thinking about new plant combinations and admiring its form and structure. Being in the garden brings me a sense of peace and well-being. However, there is just something very, very special about growing your own fruit and vegetables. And of course it can be very cost-effective. You also become more aware of eating seasonally and gain a real appreciation of how precious each crop is, and this will make you more mindful of food waste and why we should avoid this. It will be challenging at times, it involves effort and your attention needs to be brought to the tasks involved, again another meditative aspect of gardening. It is not always plain sailing and there will be testing times and failures, but when you have successes and then get to harvest your homegrown produce it is a feeling like no other.

A harvest of herbs, kale and potatoes from the garden

As with tending your garden, growing your own fruit and vegetables will get you outside and engaging with nature, whatever the weather conditions. I think that we need to give more credit to how much we benefit from the act of nurturing something. I still get a thrill when I harvest something that I have grown from seed – the tiny seed that was sown months before and that I looked after and potted on to then give me something delicious to eat. What a natural serotonin rush, I am smiling just writing about this wonder of nature.

Some highs and lows come from growing your own food. For example, I sowed eight melon seeds and they all germinated! Now, I have never grown a melon before, so this was quite a moment for me. They were tucked up in the polytunnel and when I went down to do my daily check, all of the melon seedlings had been eaten except one. Something had feasted on them during the night. I was quite upset – my vision of armfuls of delicious-tasting melons was gone. But I pulled myself together and was determined that the one remaining seedling would be saved and I would have a melon harvest, albeit smaller than anticipated, in the autumn! I brought the one remaining seedling indoors to continue growing on my kitchen windowsill. Which it did and once it reached a good strong size, I planted it out in the polytunnel. Now, I have no control over who or what will find its tender stems tasty, so it was a nervous time. Full disclosure: something ate my last remaining melon seedling. Cue feeling sorry for myself, my dream of eating homegrown melon is gone. But when you grow your own you become resilient and turn your focus onto what is doing well. In this case, I had sown some Cape Gooseberry seeds and they were doing well, so all is not lost. I had tried to grow them outside a few years ago, but they didn't manage to ripen before the shorter days and cooler weather. But now I have the polytunnel I decided to try growing them under cover. They have proven to be strong, healthy plants which the slugs don't seem to find attractive. They produce saucer-like flowers in yellow and black, then paper-like coverings which protect the growing fruit. They are ready to harvest when the covers turn from green to cream and rustle when you touch them. Inside, the fruit is a golden colour which shines like jewels. These fruits are absolutely delicious and something that you wouldn't see on the shelves of your local supermarket – exotic enough for me!

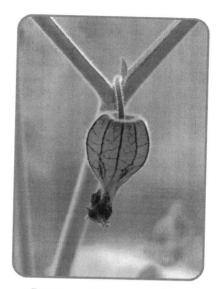

Fruit casing of the cape gooseberry

Ripe cape gooseberry fruits

Fruit

By the end of April the garden is starting to come alive, there is new growth emerging from the ground and buds appearing on the trees and shrubs. It is also time for the blossom to appear on my fruit trees and shrubs. The plum blossom has come and gone and now it is the turn of the apple blossom to burst open and give its spectacular display. Following closely behind is the blossom on the redcurrant, blackcurrant, blueberry, Lonicera and strawberries.

The plum varieties that I grow are Victoria and Jubilee which give a reliable harvest of sweet soft fruit. These are Julienne rootstock and only grow to around three metres in height, so it is still easy to prune them and gather the fruit.

I also grow four different apple varieties – Bramley Seedling (a cooker), James Grieve (a delicious eater), a Red Love (an eater with pink flesh and skin) and a cox-type apple (I am afraid that I have forgotten its name). I grow each of these fruit trees within the herbaceous borders. They are all grafted onto semi-dwarf root stock and the cox apple is a step-over grafted onto dwarf rootstock. A step-over is a fruit tree which has two lateral branches that have been trained to grow horizontally. These lateral branches are supported by posts and wires. They are great as a boundary plant and give the same amount of fruit as a standard tree. The rootstock determines the height of your fruit tree, with the semi-dwarf varieties producing the same amount of fruit as a standard tree but will only grow to around three metres in height. So, they are ideal for small to medium-sized gardens and I find that it is easier to prune them at this height and collect the fruit from them.

Blueberries are super easy to grow. They grow well in pots and as they are ericaceous plants it is easier to provide the soil conditions they prefer if they are grown in pots. For optimum pollination, you will need to have more than one plant and they should be different varieties. Once you have tasted your homegrown blueberries you will never buy shop-bought ones again. As well as being delicious, they are high in antioxidants, vitamin C and K. I also grow an edible honeysuckle called Lonicera caerulea, also high in vitamin C and A, which produces small oblong dark purple fruit that has a hint of honey in the flavour. Hence their common name of Honeyberries. They are self-pollinating, but I grow two different varieties which has improved pollination and increased the amount of fruit from each plant.

I grow my redcurrant and blackcurrant shrubs in the herbaceous border and the fruits freeze well and are delicious with yoghurt or mixed into a crumble. They are self-pollinating and will keep producing year after year without much intervention, other than a prune every year to keep an open goblet shape.

Homegrown strawberries are one of life's great pleasures, they have an intense flavour that you don't get from mass-produced fruit. Very, very easy to grow and care for, but you should replace your plants every four years to maintain fruit production. Each plant will produce runners and you can use the layering method to propagate new plants when you need to renew your old plants. Plants for free and if you like the variety then you will continue to harvest the same tasting, delicious fruits.

Their taste may not immediately make you think of fruit, but tomatoes are classed as a fruit due to their cluster of seeds held within the body of the fruit. There is something quite nostalgic about growing tomatoes – many of us will have memories of our grandparents growing these delicious fruits and I can remember the smell of the tomato plants as you brushed by them on a warm summer's day. They are easy to grow and you will get fruits with such an intense flavour, again as opposed to some commercially grown tomatoes. I grow some varieties of tomatoes in the polytunnel and others I grow in pots outside and in the raised beds. If it is a good summer with warmth and bright sunny days, then the outdoor grown tomatoes will do just as well as those under cover. As well as eating the tomatoes fresh from the vine, I will also use them to make tomato ragu sauces which I will freeze. If you don't have time to make a sauce immediately, you can freeze the tomatoes whole for use when you are ready.

Finally, the last fruit that I grow is the humble rhubarb. The crown that I have in my garden came from my grandparents' garden and is still reliably producing fruit each year. I have lifted and divided it every few years to refresh the crown – read back in Chapter 7 on how to do this. The shoots will break the ground early in the year and you will be able to harvest the stems until the end of June. Stems will still be produced after June, and you can still take the odd stem, but if you continue to remove the stems you may weaken the plant and this will affect its fruit production in future years. The stems also go a little bit stringy and tough as the season goes on. Best to harvest the young stems earlier in the summer.

Other fruits that you can grow are gooseberries and you can grow these in the borders or in a large pot. These don't need much pruning other than you keep an open goblet shape, much the same as you do for redcurrants and blackcurrants. Raspberries do well, they like a little acidity in the soil and you can give them this by mulching with an ericaceous mulch in the spring and autumn. They can be boisterous and will put out runners and you can find new plants popping up nearby. When I grew them, I dug a trench around the original plants and placed some boards in the trench which did stop the runners from appearing further down the border. Alternatively, you can grow them in large pots or raised beds solely for the raspberries.

Fruits that I grow are:

- ➤ Apples – eaters and cookers
- ➤ Plums
- ➤ Redcurrants
- ➤ Blackcurrants
- ➤ Blueberries
- ➤ Lonicera
- ➤ Strawberries
- ➤ Cape Gooseberries
- ➤ Rhubarb
- ➤ Tomatoes

Herbs

Growing your own herbs is a very cost-effective way to have fresh herbs on your doorstep. They can be grown in pots, raised beds, polytunnels, greenhouses or in your borders. I grow my Rosemary as a shrub in the border. I grow Sage in pots and place these amongst my vegetables as companion plants (more on this later in the chapter). Basil grows best under cover as it needs consistent heat and doesn't enjoy getting too wet. Sage, Rosemary, Thyme, Oregano and Marjoram are usually grown as perennials and will produce fresh leaves year on year. Soft-stemmed herbs such as Basil, Parsley, Coriander and Sorrel are treated as annuals. Sow fresh each year. I find that I get the freshest mint from sowing fresh each year, although you can grow this as a perennial. Mint can be invasive, so either have a bed only for mint or plant in a pot and then sink this into the ground. My Bay is grown in a pot as a small shrub and I pick the leaves all year round. Use these herbs fresh from the garden during the growing season, but you can also dry the herbs or freeze them so you have them to hand all year round. Surplus harvests can be prepared and frozen so that you can enjoy them throughout the winter.

Herbs that I grow are:

- ➤ Chives
- ➤ Sweet basil
- ➤ Thai basil
- ➤ Parsley
- ➤ Coriander
- ➤ Sorrel
- ➤ Thyme

- Bay
- Rosemary
- Mint
- Sage
- Wild garlic
- Lemon balm
- Lemon verbena

Vegetables

I remember the first vegetables that I grew were carrots and I filled a pot with compost and sowed some carrot seeds. A few months later I had actual carrots! What a thrill and they were delicious. I had the grow-your-own bug from that moment. The thrill of eating something that I had grown from seed has not left me. From there I started to grow other vegetables and I still get the same thrill from going into the garden and collecting a selection of vegetables that will go into the evening meal. I am by no means self-sufficient, but there is enough produce to provide food for many months of the year.

It is not all plain sailing and you will come across some challenges, but don't be downhearted if you have 'failures' – this happens. Later in this chapter, I will talk about preventative measures you can take to get good, healthy crops of vegetables as well as steps you can take to counteract any losses you might suffer.

I grow the vegetables that I like to eat regularly and those that I find difficult to source in the supermarket. I also like to try growing something new to me each year – this year it is the small snowball turnip. If it is a success, I will grow it again next year.

Vegetables that I grow are:

- Potatoes
- Chard
- Spinach
- Dwarf green kale
- Leeks
- Courgettes
- Celery
- Onions
- Shallots
- Peas
- Green beans
- Sweetcorn
- Carrots
- Turnip

Growing from seed

I now grow all my vegetable plants from seed. I understand that this may not be possible for everyone as you will need a bit of space – although a windowsill is ideal for the germination of your seeds – and you will need some equipment. I find that growing from seed is very cost-effective, with a packet of seeds costing only a couple of pounds to buy.

We looked at growing perennials from seed in Chapter 5; the method for sowing, germinating, pricking out, potting on and planting is the same for vegetables. If you are planning on growing your vegetables from seed and growing them until they are big enough to be planted out, then please refer back to Chapter 5 and follow the process described there. I always grow my vegetables indoors and undercover, growing them on until they have a large root system and I feel they are big enough to withstand some predation by the ever-present gastropods!

Sowing vegetable seeds directly into the ground

Alternatively, vegetable seeds can also be directly sown into your borders, raised beds, planters or pots. Using this method will remove the need for germinating seeds indoors and potting on prior to going into the garden. I have outlined the process below.

Equipment

- Fork
- Rake
- Soil conditioner or compost
- Seed packet
- A cane or similar to make a drill
- Watering can with rose

Method

➤ Remove any large stones and break up any compacted soil. To give the seeds the best chance to germinate, the soil should have a texture similar to breadcrumbs or as near as you can get it.

➤ Prepare the area that you will be sowing your seeds into by adding some nutrient-rich compost or soil conditioner. Lightly fork this in. Some vegetable seeds, such as carrots, don't like to be grown in newly fertilised soil, so always check the packet before you prepare the ground as this will give you guidelines on what your chosen vegetable seeds prefer.

➤ Check your seed packet to find out when you should sow seeds outdoors.

- ➤ The seed packet should also tell you how deep your seeds should be sown.
- ➤ If you are sowing your seeds in a row, create a drill to the required depth. I use a cane or run my finger along the soil to create the drill.
- ➤ If you are sowing larger seeds, spinach, for example, you can place these individually along the drill. Leave space between each seed.
- ➤ If the seeds you are sowing are smaller, carrots for example, then put the seeds into the palm of one hand and pick up a small amount with the fingers of your other hand. Sprinkle the seeds finely along the drill.
- ➤ With your fingers now push the soil from either side of the drill over the seeds.
- ➤ Now water in, using a watering can with a rose.
- ➤ Keep the soil moist as the heat of the sun and the moisture will all encourage the seeds to germinate.
- ➤ Once your seedlings have germinated and the true leaves have unfurled, you can look and see if the seedlings need to be thinned out.
- ➤ Again, using the information on your seed packet, check the spacing that your vegetable

needs between plants. This will inform how much thinning of seedlings you need to carry out. Pick a strong-looking seedling and remove any others that are crowding around it. Work your way along the row until you have individual seedlings with the required growing space.

Succession planting

This is the staggered sowing of crops, which avoids a glut of a crop. Basically, sow some, then a few weeks later sow again, repeat as many times as you need to. The crops will mature in a succession so you can eat continuously without them all arriving at the same time. It also means that you will have some back-up seedlings if any are eaten by slugs/snails etc.

Growing from plug plants

You can also grow vegetables from plug plants which you can buy from nurseries, garden centres or online. These have been sown by the supplier and will be ready for purchasing once they have their true leaves and a good root system. You can plant these straight out into your garden or you can pot them into 9 cm or 11 cm pots to grow larger before you plant them out.

Growing potatoes

Why am I singling out growing potatoes, you may ask. Potatoes are grown from what is called a seed potato. As well as different varieties of potatoes to choose to grow, you will also see that you can choose from first earlies, second earlies and main crop potatoes. I thought I would just run through some of the main things to be aware of when growing potatoes.

Seed potatoes are specially grown potatoes that are certified as virus-free which should ensure that you get a healthy crop of potatoes. They will be delivered to you as individual tubers and are normally packaged by the kilogram.

Chitting potatoes is not necessary, but chitting your potatoes will encourage the tubers to produce strong, short, fat green shoots before you plant them out. Doing this will give the tuber a head start going into the ground. When my seed potatoes arrive, I take them out of their packaging and place them in an old egg box. I then place these egg boxes in a cool light room – out of direct sunshine – and leave them to produce their small shoots.

Potatoes chitting in egg boxes

So many varieties of seed potato are available and it really is a matter of personal choice as to which one you choose. I prefer a potato with a waxy flesh and smooth shape, so when I choose my seed potatoes I will look for varieties that have these characteristics.

First early potatoes tend to be smaller potatoes, often described as salad potatoes. They mature between 60-110 days after planting. These are best eaten fresh from picking them and don't store well. Best eaten boiled with melted butter in early summer.

Second early potatoes will be slightly larger in size when you receive them. These mature a few weeks after the first early potatoes. Again, these are best eaten fresh from the garden. These are my favourite type of potato. They are still relatively small if you pick them in July, so very much the same as the first earlies in flavour and simply boiled with melted butter, lovely. But you can leave these in the ground or in bags for a good couple of months and they will continue to grow. I like to have them boiled or roasted and added to curries.

Maincrop potatoes are larger and will need a bit more space to grow as they will produce larger potatoes. They take around 140 days to mature and will be ready from late August. These potatoes are good for boiling, roasting and baking. Maincrop potatoes will normally store well if kept in a dark, frost-free environment.

Planting out potatoes – growing in the ground

Your potatoes will have arrived with a label and normally this label will give you guidelines for when to plant them out. A rough guide is from the end of March to early April. But as we have discussed, timings will very much depend on where you live and the conditions in your garden. A rough rule of thumb is once your soil has started to warm up. To test this, dig down into the soil with your hand and gauge if the soil is warm. If it's still very cold, delay putting the potatoes in for another week and try again.

The ground that you are planting your potatoes into should have had a good layer of compost, well-rotted manure or soil conditioner lightly forked into it.

Potatoes should be planted deeply, around six inches deep, leave around 12 inches between each tuber (15 inches for maincrop potatoes). When you see the leaf shoots above the ground you should cover these – this is called earthing up. When the leaves break ground again, you can earth up again. There are reasons for doing this: firstly, it is to protect the young shoots from any late frosts; secondly, potatoes exposed to light will turn green and cannot be eaten; and lastly, it is to increase your crop, you now have the potatoes growing under a deep layer of soil.

Keep the potatoes well watered – the growing tubers need moisture in order to swell and grow. You can also give them a liquid feed rich in nitrogen – if you have made nettle feed then this is ideal.

Check if your potatoes are ready to harvest when they have been in the recommended number of days (see above). To do this, use your hand to dig down and find a potato. If it still feels quite small, then leave them to grow on for another week and check again.

Lift your potatoes from the ground very carefully using a fork. Put the fork in the ground near to the potato plant and lever upwards; the leaves and the potatoes nearest the top will loosen from the ground first. Keep digging until you have all the potatoes out of the ground and move onto the next plant. Just be very careful not to spear the potatoes. If the soil is very loose, you can use your hands to lift the potatoes out of the ground.

Planting out potatoes – growing in bags

I grow my potatoes in bags as I like to keep the other beds free for my other vegetables. Growing potatoes this way will mean that you will have to buy potting compost to fill the bags.

I fill the potato bag with compost to around three inches from the bottom, then I place three tubers, gently resting them on the compost with their shoots facing upwards. I then cover the potatoes to fill the bag to around halfway. Give the bag a good water and then check for signs that the leaf shoots are appearing through the compost. When they do, I add more compost to cover the leaves. When the leaves next break the surface of the soil, I add compost to just before the top of the bag.

Keep the soil moist – the bags will dry out much quicker than the soil in your raised beds or borders.

I get really good crops growing my potatoes in bags, although you can get bigger crops from growing directly into the ground. To harvest your potatoes, you can tip the bag out and remove the potatoes. I sprinkle the used compost onto my compost heap – I sift it to make sure that there are not tiny potato tubers in there; if there are, I remove them. If you don't need all of the potatoes in a bag, just dig down with your hand and remove the potatoes that you need. Make sure you cover up the potatoes that are left in the bag.

I love being able to pop down to the end of the garden and dig up a few potatoes that will be cooked within hours of harvesting.

Where to grow your vegetables

It doesn't matter how much space you have, if you want to grow your own vegetables, herbs and fruit then you can. They can be grown in the ground, in raised beds, planters or pots. Give them the right conditions and you will get a harvest. You may have a greenhouse or polytunnel – these allow you to have a longer growing period as you are growing under cover. If you are able to heat them, then you are also able to start your germination process off much sooner. I don't heat my polytunnel, but I have found that I can grow herbs and spinach, chard and kale throughout the winter months, which suits me.

Growing vegetables in the ground will involve you making sure that the soil is nourished by adding well-rotted manure, soil conditioner or homemade compost. Remove any large stones as this will impede germination and growth. Break up any large clumps of soil – again, this will provide a crumbly textured soil for the vegetable plants. Avoid walking over the ground as this will create compaction which will make it harder for the plants to germinate and put down roots. If you do have to move around the ground, then consider standing on a plank of wood whilst working around the plants.

Raised beds are ideal if, like me, you have very heavy clay soil. I built my raised beds using old decking boards measuring one metre across and around three metres in length. You should never stand in a raised bed as you will compact the soil – that's why having your raised beds around one metre wide and being able to access them from both sides is ideal as you won't need to step into the bed. My raised beds are two decking boards high, which allows enough depth for root vegetables, and as you will be filling them with compost it will cut down on how much you need to fill the bed. To fill the raised beds, I put a layer of small dry clippings from shrubs on the base, then I added a layer of leaves. Both of these will eventually break down. I also added old compost from pots and growing potatoes in the bottom. The top two-thirds of your raised bed should be filled with nutrient-rich compost. Every year before I put my vegetable plants into the raised bed, I lightly fork the top of the soil and remove any old roots from last year's crops. I then sprinkle some homemade compost over the top of the bed to refresh the nutrient value of the soil. You can buy soil conditioner or well-rotted manure which will do the same job if you don't have your own compost.

Planters come in various shapes and sizes. Make sure that they have enough drainage holes in them and I line them with weed control fabric to stop the wood from coming into contact with the compost and it prolongs the life of wooden planters. Like the raised beds, the bottom third can be made up of leaves or compost from the previous year. The remaining two-thirds will be nutrient-rich compost.

Pots are ideal for growing herbs in. Make sure the drainage hole is not blocked, cover it with some crock and add your compost. If you are growing annual herbs in a pot, you can put the compost in your compost heap, clean the pot out and tuck it away until you need it next year. I grow my Bay in a large pot and each spring I scrape away the top layer of compost and add a fresh layer. This boosts the nutrients in the pot which will feed your plant.

Growing in a polytunnel allows you to extend your growing season. You can sow your seeds a little earlier, grow them on before planting them out and it also means that you can grow crops through the winter months. In my polytunnel I have a raised bed on either side of the door which runs along the length of the tunnel. I refresh the soil in the raised beds every spring, just as I do for my outside raised beds. I have staging in the polytunnel on which I lay a piece of plyboard. This is where my seedlings grow and when I pot them on, they continue to live in the polytunnel until the weather is warm enough for them to be planted outside. I take the staging out when I start to grow vegetables and fruit in the beds below.

A greenhouse is also a great space that allows you to extend the growing season as with the polytunnel. Some people only use them to germinate and grow seedlings. Others will be able to plant into raised beds or straight into the ground – if the greenhouse is situated over soil.

Have a plan

Each autumn I go through my seed collection and check the seeds are still within their best sown-by date. Any that are outside that date I will dispose of. If stored properly, seeds will stay fresh for years and it is ok to use seeds outside the recommended sow-by date, but you may find that the rate of germination is lower than you would get from using fresh seeds. Then, on a piece of paper, I will list everything I want to grow in the coming year, vegetables as well as any annuals, biennials and perennials. And then I create a separate list of any seeds that I need to buy for the coming year. Alternatively, seed swapping or sharing with other gardeners is a great way to save money on buying seeds. You may get a handful of seeds of a vegetable or certain variety that you can try and grow before you buy your own packet of seeds. Look out for local announcements via social media or ask at your local allotments.

I use an old diary to sketch out where I will be growing my vegetables in the coming year. This sketch includes the polytunnel, raised beds, pots, planters and bags. I will then look back at the sketch I created in the previous year, detailing where I grew my vegetables. When it comes to your fixed beds, i.e. not your planters, pots or bags as you can renew the compost in these, it's important to keep a record of where you planted your vegetables as you will need to rotate some of your crops. More on crop rotation later in the chapter.

The next step is to list the seeds that I will be sowing. Beside this there is a column where I will write down when I plan to sow these seeds. Further down the line I will also note when they germinated, when I potted them on, and when they were planted out into the garden. This is not essential, but I like to keep a record to compare dates in the coming years.

Finally, I write on the sketch where I plan to grow the vegetables, herbs and flowering plants. The sketch is a very useful visual aid to remind me of my grand planting plan! There are often changes along the way – perhaps one of my crops won't germinate as well as I had hoped, and the smaller crop will be moved into a different position, or I may get a bigger crop germinating and I will have to shuffle some plants around to accommodate this. But as a starting point it's good to have a plan.

I use an old diary to note what I will be growing, when to sow and then a sketch of where they will eventually be planted

Crop rotation

Where you are planting your vegetable crops into raised beds or directly into the ground in designated growing beds, it is important to rotate your crops. This means moving your crops one place on, each year. That's why having a record of where you have planted your crops is important. Why rotate crops? It will help to maintain soil health, improve and enhance the nutrients in the soil, and also help to deter soil-borne pests and diseases. For example, plants in the brassica family can be susceptible to club root disease, and those in the onion family can suffer from white rot. Plants in the potato and root families are very good at improving soil structure by breaking up compacted soil. This is very useful if you are planting directly into a border. Plants in each of the families have different nutritional needs and will also add to the nutrient levels having been grown in an area of ground.

I have listed below the plant families and given examples of crops that are part of each of the families. There is also a list of crops which don't need to be part of your crop rotation plan and can be grown anywhere within your rotated crops.

Crop families

Brassicas – Brussels sprouts, cabbage, cauliflower, kale, kohlrabi, oriental greens, radish, swede and turnip

Legumes – peas, broad beans, French beans and runner beans

Potato – potatoes, tomatoes, peppers and aubergines

Onion – onions, leeks, garlic and shallots

Root – beetroot, carrot, celeriac, celery, fennel, parsley and parsnip

The following crops don't need to be part of your crop rotation plan and can be planted anywhere in your scheme:

Courgettes, pumpkins, squashes, marrows, cucumber, salad leaves and sweetcorn

I have added a couple of website addresses in the reference section of this book where you can read more about crop rotation.

Companion Planting

Companion planting is when you plant different crops or plants near each other. This is done in order to suppress weeds by covering any exposed soil. It will also aid pollination, deter pests and lead to an increase in crop productivity.

You can plant quick growing crops such as lettuce or radish amongst your onions and shallots as they will mature and be harvested before the onions and shallots put on a lot of leaf growth and shade them out. You can save space by planting crops at the base of any vertical crops such as beans, peas or sweetcorn. Try planting courgettes or squashes at the base of these plants.

I also plant herbs and flowering plants around my crops as they attract pollinators and deter pests from my crops.

I have listed just a few of the companion plants you might like to consider growing alongside your vegetable crops. If nothing else, they add some lovely vibrant colour to your vegetable borders.

▩ List of Companion Plants

Calendula or Marigold – will attract aphids and the sticky substance on their leaves will trap the aphid.

Viper's-bugloss – this attracts pollinators such as bees, wasps and butterflies.

Phacelia – this is known as a green compost which can be planted after the crop has been harvested and dug into the soil after flowering. It attracts pollinators and also adds nitrogen to the soil.

Poppies – will attract pollinators such as the wasp which in turn will predate on aphids.

Sage – will deter snails, carrot root fly and flea beetles.

Lavender – bees love lavender but little else does, so it is good to grow alongside your vegetables to deter other insects.

Borage – attracts pollinators; slugs and snails will avoid where it is growing.

Mint – because of its strong odour many insects and bugs will avoid mint.

Artemisia or Wormwood – this is a really useful plant as it will deter ants, carrot root flies, cabbage maggots, flea beetles, whiteflies and codling moths.

Basil – the strong scent of basil will deter whitefly and carrot fly.

Nasturtiums – deter flea and cucumber beetles. The cabbage moth loves it and will lay its eggs on the nasturtium rather than your cabbages.

Chives – planting near to carrots will deter carrot root fly, as will onions and garlic.

Chrysanthemum – will repel insects such as aphids, leafhoppers and spider mites.

Hyssop – will attract the cabbage moth which will in turn help out your brassicas.

Feeding your crops

If you are growing your vegetables in the ground or raised beds, it is important to nourish and regenerate the soil before you plant your new vegetable plants. I loosen the soil by lightly forking over the top of the soil, breaking up any compacted soil. Rake this over to create a surface area that is level. I then add a thin layer of homemade compost. If you don't have this, then a peat-free soil conditioner or well-rotted manure is also good. Give this new layer a light rake over and break up any compacted pieces.

If you are growing your vegetables in planters or pots you can remove the majority of the old compost – this can be added to the compost heap, you can leave the last third of the old compost as the plants will only access the top two-thirds of the soil and this is where you want to have fresh new compost containing all the nutrients.

As the crops mature and grow, they will be taking up the nutrients from the compost and accessing the nitrogen in the soil. I always recommend giving vegetable crops a liquid feed every week once the flowering and pollination has happened and the plants start to produce their crop. I use my comfrey tea for this job, but you can also use seaweed feed and you can buy liquid feed from your nursery or garden centre. Granular feed such as fish blood and bone can also be used to feed the plants – sprinkle this around the plant, lightly fork in and then water.

Watering your crops

Vegetable plants like consistency in their access to water, but as you know our weather doesn't tend to do consistency! The general rule of thumb is that if there hasn't been any rain for 10-14 days then you should give your vegetable plants a drink of water. If you are growing your vegetables in the ground or raised beds, then they will have access to water deeper down below the surface, so before you water, dig down with your hand and see if the soil is damp or dry. Overwatering can cause too much green growth to the detriment of flowering and producing the crop. Too little and the yet-to-be pollinated flowers can drop and you lose a potential pea, bean or courgette. Tomato fruits can split if the conditions fluctuate from dry to wet and vice versa. If you are growing your crops in planters, pots or bags, you will have to water more frequently in dry weather as the plants only have access to the water within where they are being grown. I check my planters and pots every couple of days and water if the soil is dry below the surface.

To try and reduce the need for watering, keep the area around your plants weed-free, as weeds take up a good amount of moisture themselves. If you use companion planting, you will be covering most of the exposed soil with those plants which also reduces evaporation. You can cover the soil with a black weed control fabric – this allows water to permeate the soil and reduces evaporation. You plant your crops by cutting a small cross in the fabric and placing your plant in the hole in the fabric. In Chapter 8 I talked about using the Olla method to water your plants, which is very effective. You can also buy what are called leaky pipes or drip watering systems. These provide a consistent flow of water to your plants and are very useful if you are away from the garden for any length of time. They can be controlled by timers.

Protecting your crops

It's not only us growers who love our fruit and vegetable crops – there are insects, bugs, gastropods, birds, squirrels, rabbits and sometimes even our beloved pets! Believe me, I know how upsetting it is to have your lovingly grown plants nibbled on. For example, last year I had a lovely crop of blueberries on one of my plants and they needed another week to fully ripen. I would harvest them when I came back from a week away. And, yes, you've guessed it – every single blueberry was gone when I came back. A squirrel had taken them! Why didn't I have the plant netted? Because we have never had squirrels in our garden, but one had started to visit the garden and was as keen as I was to pick those juicy fruits. So, this year, the soft fruits in the garden will be netted.

Netting

This can be used to cover your soft fruit plants such as blueberries, redcurrants and raspberries. You can build a frame and cover this with the netting, secure it with twine or wire, or lay the netting directly over the plant. Always make sure that the netting is taut to avoid birds getting tangled in it. You can also build a frame around your raised beds and cover with netting to protect your vegetable crops.

Cloches

These are normally made of rigid plastic and are shaped like a half-moon; these can be laid over your plants to protect them and will be transparent, which allows sunlight to reach your plants. They can also be used to help seeds germinate as they will stop the cold air or frost reaching the seedlings and young plants, meaning you can sow a little earlier in the season or protect plants if a late overnight frost is forecast.

Fleece

Horticultural fleece allows sunlight and rain to filter through it, making it a really useful piece of kit to have in your shed. I use it in the polytunnel to cover the crops over the winter as the polytunnel isn't heated and the fleece provides some protection from the cold temperatures. I will also cover my seedlings in it overnight until the temperatures rise and the polytunnel retains the daytime heat. You can also use it outside in the beds or raised beds to provide some protection from frost and also from predation from bugs, insects and birds. Like netting, you can lay it directly over your crops or build a frame and secure the netting to the frame.

Harvesting

The moment we have all been looking forward to: your crops are ready to harvest! From seed to plate, the time has come.

The harvesting schedule in our garden goes something like this...rhubarb, strawberries, peas, honeyberries, courgettes, spinach and chard, basil, second early potatoes, French beans, tomatoes, redcurrants, blackcurrants, onions, shallots, runner beans, plums, blueberries, sweetcorn, celery, cape gooseberries, autumn fruiting raspberries, apples, leeks, main crop potatoes and turnips.

At the start of this chapter we talked about the benefits of having a plan and we looked at noting what we were going to grow, when to sow and when to pot on etc. It is also useful, especially if you are just starting on the grow-your-own-food journey, to note down when each of your crops should be ready to harvest. You can get this information from the seed packet, but bear in mind that this is just a guide as your harvesting time will depend on where you are in the country, your garden's own climate and what the weather was like when you were growing your crops. And, failing all that research, a visual check is always the most reliable – oh, and a taste test!

Top 7 tips for growing your own fruit and vegetables

1. Grow what you like to eat, start with one type of vegetable, fruit or herb and build up your repertoire from there.

2. Always read the labels on your seed packets for guidance as to when to sow, when to plant out and when to harvest. But remember that your garden has its own climate and adjust your timings accordingly. And, keep your seed packet for future reference.

3. You can grow your fruit and vegetables in any space, large or small, in a container or raised bed as well as directly into the ground.

4. Your fruit and vegetables will need access to water and fed regularly. Always check the

feeding and watering needs of each crop to make sure you are giving them what they need.

5. Know your crop families and follow a crop rotation cycle to avoid infestations, disease and maintain your soil health.

6. Companion planting will help you save on watering and weeding. It will also aid pollination and can deter infestations from your crops.

7. Enjoy your harvests! You have earned it, you've sown the seed, nurtured the plant and now you get to eat the freshest and tastiest fruit and vegetables you have ever eaten.

I hope that I have given you the confidence to start growing your own fruit and vegetables. It is not always plain sailing, but it really is exciting and fulfilling to eat what you have grown from seed or plug plant. I do believe that homegrown fruit and vegetables taste better than commercially grown alternatives. You can eat your produce fresh, or dry it – in the case of herbs – and freeze it to enjoy on a cold winter's day. Give it a go, and let me know how you get on.

Notes

_____

_____

_____

_____

_____

_____

_____

_____

_____

_____

_____

_____

_____

_____

_____

_____

_____

_____

Chapter Ten

Designing Your Garden Layout

"No single sort of garden suits everyone. Shut your eyes and dream of the garden you'd most love to open your eyes and start planting. Loved gardens flourish, boring ones are hard work."

Jackie French

"My garden is my most beautiful masterpiece."

Claude Monet

In 2010 I moved into a new house which came with a large garden – well, it wasn't a garden, it was an expanse of soil surrounded by a fence!

Here is a photograph of the garden in 2010...

The garden in 2010

How exciting and also daunting! I had for the first time a blank canvas to work on as all my previous gardens were already established when I moved in. But where to start? This chapter is all about introducing you to some of the things to think about when it comes to planning the layout of your garden space. Big or small, blank canvas or established, the concepts and key things to consider are the same.

Before we start working on our sketch, let's have a quick look at zoning...

Zoning

Zoning your garden is about sectioning up your garden into areas – where to sit, where to entertain, where to play and work etc. It is also thinking about where to place certain plants – herbs for cooking placed near to the kitchen area and scented plants where you will be able to make the most of them. So, when you start to work on your sketch, keep these zones in mind and it will help you to decide where to place your chosen areas within your garden space. Now to the sketch...

The Sketch

For me it all starts with a pencil, ruler, eraser and paper. I can visualise the end product much better when I write things down or sketch them by hand. Whereas, I know many other people find using the computer based design tools much easier to use and help them plan their layout. Whatever you are more comfortable using, go for it.

Before going any further, I would say that this exercise can be carried out on any garden, whether it is established or a blank canvas. What we are doing here is thinking of how you would like your garden space laid out. Once you know what you would like you can then note where changes are to be made if you have an existing garden.

When I am designing new borders or layouts for clients, I sketch out how the garden is laid out at present, I then tape a piece of tracing paper over this sketch and draw the new layout or new planting scheme onto the tracing paper. It is easy then to see the current layout and then overlay your plans for the new layout. You can also take a series of photographs of the garden, print them out and then add a layer of tracing paper to sketch your new ideas onto the layout.

Start by drawing the boundaries of your garden space, add in the position of your house and any gates or access areas. Have your climate map to hand as it will come in useful when you are deciding where to place borders, seating areas, vegetable beds etc.

Now sit quietly – this can be anywhere, but I would find it more useful to do this exercise either sitting in the garden or where I could see the garden. Close your eyes and bring to mind an image of how you would like your garden to look. Watch yourself move around the garden. Ask yourself some of these questions and write down the answers that come to you.

Questions to ask

- Where would you like to sit in the morning and again in the evening?
- Are there any areas where you want privacy or want to add height to the garden?
- Where would you like the garden beds to be situated, where they get the best light and you can see them and appreciate them?

- Think of how you want to move about the garden – these are your paths/walkway
- What shape will your paths be, linear or curved?
- What materials will the paths be made of?
- How much of a seating/entertainment space do you need?
- Where will this entertainment space be situated? Will it be near the house or further down the garden in a secluded area? Do you have small children or pets that you need to cater for when using the garden? What needs to be in place for them?
- Where will you dry your laundry? Will you use drying poles or a rotary dryer? Where is this best placed?
- Where do you need height or privacy?
- If you need access to water in the garden, where will you put the tap or hose?
- If you are collecting rainwater, where will you place your water butt or water tank?
- If you want to have outbuildings such as a shed, greenhouse or polytunnel, where are these best placed? Take into account ease of use, how often you will be using them and also access to light.

- If you have an established garden, what needs to be removed, moved or changed to fit with your new layout?

You now have your first draft of your new layout, and this is your starting point for making changes. You can always alter the layout, it isn't written in stone. Use it to refer to, go back and edit as ideas come to you. The idea of the sketch is to help you plan the layout. The hard landscaping is the key and the backbone of any design. Get this right and in place, then all the rest will fall into place.

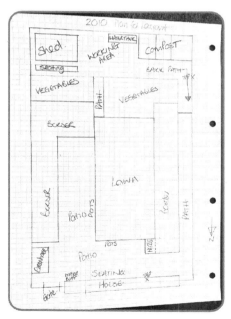

A sketch of the layout of my garden

I have included a picture of the sketch I made when I was designing the layout of the garden. This shows where the paths were to be placed, where the lawn and flower borders would be, and also noted where the seating and patio areas would be built.

This is the finished sketch, although there were several earlier versions of the layout sketch as I continued to add to and amend some of my initial thoughts and ideas. Things such as finalising the sizes of the borders and pathways, adding a patio area in the working area of the garden as I realised I wanted to expand the area I would grow fruit and vegetables in. The compost area was always going to be at the bottom of the garden, but until I had sketched out where the shed and working area would be I couldn't place the compost heap. This all led to the eventual placement of the tap and hoses – one at each end of the garden – which in turn led to a water butt and water tank being added to the layout. Since then, the polytunnel has been added and several more raised beds. But they all came from this original layout drawing.

The plan

Anyone who knows me knows how much I love a list! So for me the next thing to do is to create a planning list; this would include:

- What needs to be done?
- Can the work be carried out in phases, what are these phases?
- When does it need to be done by?
- What is the order that the tasks need to be carried out in?
- What is my budget?
- What do I need to buy or obtain?
- Can I recycle or repurpose anything?
- Can I carry out the tasks myself or do I need to call in help?

As with all lists, this is a working document and you will amend it, add to it and the most satisfying part – what can you tick off the list as having been done!

The Plants

I might be wrong, but I think this is the bit that really excites people – choosing or planning your planting scheme. This doesn't need to be carried out in one hit, but can be started and built on over the coming months and years. The subject of planning and designing your planting schemes is a subject that will definitely fill another book on its own! But here I will give you some pointers as to what to think about when planning your planting scheme.

What to consider when planning your planting scheme

- ➤ Remember that the planting and the layout of your garden space should suit your needs and bring you pleasure.
- ➤ Have your climate map handy to refer to so that you can see what the growing conditions are in each of the areas in your garden.
- ➤ List or mark the plants that you want to keep.
- ➤ List or mark the plants that you want to remove.
- ➤ List or mark the plants that you want to keep but move to another position.
- ➤ I use different coloured twine or wool to mark plants for keeping, moving etc – this is a useful visual aid.
- ➤ What plants would you like more of?
- ➤ Note where you would like more height in the garden for privacy or screening.
- ➤ What colours do you like to see in the garden? Don't forget green, this is as important as all the other colours as it will fill the gaps in between flowering and throughout the seasons.

- ➤ Different coloured and shaped leaves also add interest into a planting scheme, think about this when you are choosing your plants.
- ➤ Do you want scented plants? Where would you like these to be placed?
- ➤ What plants would you like that will give you interest in the spring, summer, autumn and winter?
- ➤ What plants will provide you with structure in the garden? Look at shrubs for this, they can be evergreen or deciduous.
- ➤ Some deciduous shrubs and trees will give you lovely stem interest during the winter season.
- ➤ Texture is also an important feature of some plants; grasses will give you movement as well as being soft to the touch.
- ➤ Ask around, you might find that people are giving away plants that you might want for your garden. Plant swaps are very popular and help to save money.
- ➤ If you buy one plant, can you grow more by collecting their seeds or taking cuttings? This will increase your stock.

➤ Would you like bulbs in the garden? They
provide colour in the spring border, filling
gaps until the perennials start to put on
growth.

➤ You can add height by installing an obelisk or
making your own tall structure and growing a
climber up them.

➤ Save money by buying smaller plants and
watch them grow over the coming years.

➤ Grow your own annuals and biennials and
they will fill any gaps in the borders.

A garden is always changing, both from season to
season but also from year to year. Look for inspiration
from other gardens, your friends and family's gardens.
Use books or the internet to give you ideas for plants
and how to put your scheme together. Don't rush it,
take your time and enjoy the journey of creating your
garden space. Make a start, even if it is just one plant.

And finally...

Here are photographs of the garden today...14 years on.
The pathways and patios are still where I had sketched
them all those years ago and I am so glad that I took the
time to really think about them. Bringing the border in
from the boundary fence and placing a path at the back
of the border has worked so well. I can work this border

from both sides. Because of the levels in the garden I couldn't do this for the border on the other side of the garden, but I didn't make the border too wide and can work it from the patio. I have placed a small informal path that runs through the border lower down on the left to allow me easy access to this border. The planting has been changed over the years and will continue to be changed, plants moved, new planting put in. That's the joy of a garden. The vegetable growing areas have multiplied over the years as I have really loved growing my own food, but the 'allotment' area is still where I planned it to be. It's a busy garden, but I love it. I love the challenges that it brings, the excitement I get from changing the planting schemes or adding new plants, colour and structure.

A garden is always a work in progress. Your use of the garden will change over time and the layout may change to reflect this. Ultimately, enjoy it, you've earned it! Now sit and enjoy your garden space, take in the sounds, the scents and the view.

*The garden as it is today. Photograph
taken in the summer from above*

*The garden as it is today. Photograph
taken in the winter from above*

Top 7 tips for designing your garden layout

1. Carve your garden up into zones – where you would like to sit, entertain, play and work. Where would you like your borders or vegetable beds?

2. Sketch your garden, starting with the boundaries and any existing structures such as a shed or greenhouse. Use a computer-based design tool or a pencil and paper.

3. Close your eyes and imagine what the garden you want will look like. Imagine yourself moving around the garden, where the paths will be, the borders etc.

4. If you have an existing garden, sketch the layout you already have then lay a piece of tracing paper over the top and now sketch how you would like the garden to be laid out.

5. You should be thinking about the pathways, seating and entertainment areas. Where the working area will be, or if you have children where the area for play will be. Amenities such as access to water or water collection

areas should be planned as well as any storage areas needed.

6. Document your plan – what needs to be done, when and by whom. What is your budget? How can you save money – repurposing or recycling items, asking for help or swapping plants and materials. What is the order of events and when do you plan to carry out the work?

7. What plants would you like to see in the garden? What plants do you want more of, want to remove or move to another area? Can you grow any plants from seed? Is plant swapping or re-homing plants an option? Take your time, this can be done in stages.

Notes

Plant Names

When mentioning plant names throughout this book, I have in the main used their common names, but here I have listed the common names as well as their Latin names as a guide for you. The Latin naming convention allows the plant genus and species to be listed and can help when we are looking for a particular variety of plant.

Common plant name	Latin name
Columbine	*Aquilegia vulgaris*
Smoketree	*Cotinus*
Yarrow	*Achillea millefolium*
Marigold/Tagete	*Calendula officinalis*
Sedum	*Hylotelephium*
Cosmos	*Cosmos bipinnatus*
Photinia Red Robin	*Photinia x fraseri*
Tussock grass	*Deschampsia cespitosa*
Daylily	*Hemerocallis fulva*
Honesty	*Lunaria*
Delphinium	*Delphinium elatum*
Daffodil	*Narcissus*

Field Scabious	*Knautia*
Hellebore	*Helleborus orientalis*
Oxeye Daisy	*Leucanthemum*
Lupin	*Lupinus*
Peony	*Paeonia lactiflora*
Catmint	*Nepeta*
Lavender	*Lavendula*
Blueberries	*Vaccinium sect. Cyanococcus*
Azalea	*Rhododendron*
Pieris	*Pieris japonica*
Plantain lilies	*Hosta*
Plum tree	*Prunus domestica*
Silene flos-cuculi	*Ragged Robin*
Maple	*Acer palmatum*
Lilac	*Syringa*
Bell flower	*Campanula*
Fern	*Tracheophyta*
Red Hot Pokers	*Kniphofia*
Montbretia	*Crocosmia*
Dogwood	*Cornus*
Jasmine	*Jasminum*
Honeysuckle	*Lonicera*
Hazel	*Hamamelis*
Primrose	*Primula vulgaris*
Tobacco plant	*Nicotiana*
Zinnia	*Zinnia elegans*
Sunflower	*Helianthus*
Poppy	*Papaver*
Nasturtium	*Tropaeolum*

Viper's-bugloss	*Echium vulgare*
White Laceflower	*Orlaya grandiflora*
Love in a Mist	*Nigella*
Toadflax	*Linaria maroccana*
Bishop's flower	*Ammi majus*
Cornflower	*Centaurea cyanus*
Scabious	*Scabiosa*
Hattie's pincushion	*Astrantia*
Fleabane	*Erigeron*
Beardtongues	*Penstemon*
Geranium	*Pelargonium*
Vervain	*Verbena officinalis*
Butterfly bush	*Buddleia*
Hydrangea	*Hortensia*
Fuchsia	*Fuchsia*
Forsythia	*Forsythia x intermedia*
Mock orange	*Philadelphus*
Willow	*Salix*
Iris	*Iris*
Michaelmas daisy	*Aster*
Sea holly	*Eryngium*
Flowering quince	*Chaenomeles speciosa*
Apple tree	*Malus domestica*
Crab apple	*Malus sylvestris*
Sweet Rocket	*Hesperis*
Evening Primrose	*Oenothera biennis*
Forget-me-not	*Myosotis sylvatica*
Flowering Cherry tree	*Prunus*
Geum	*Geum*

Rose	*Rosa*
Snapdragon	*Antirrhinum*
Cup and Saucer Vine	*Cobaea*
Spider flower	*Cleome*
Prostrate pigweed	*Amaranthus*
Snow in summer	*Alyssum*
Carnation, Pink or Sweet William	*Dianthus*
Hollyhocks	*Malvaceae*
Geranium	*Pelagorium*
River lily or Crimson flag lily	*Hesperanta*
Cone flowers or Black eyed Susan	*Rudbeckia*
Elder	*Sambucus*
Japanese rose	*Kerria*
Knitbone	*Comfrey*
Borago officianalis	*Borage*
Scorpion weed	*Phacelia*
Wormwood	*Artemisia*
Korean mint	*Hyssop*

Conclusion

"The soul cannot thrive in the absence of a garden."

Thomas Moore

Here we are at the end of this book, this handbook which I really hope you will have as your gardening companion. We have travelled far together, from looking at some of the terms used in gardening, to discovering how to make your garden space a haven for wildlife and how to grow your own fruit and vegetables. I hope that I have ignited your passion for gardening and that you gain some of the physical and wellbeing benefits that being outside in nature can bring you.

My passion is for gardening and growing plants and food, but more than that, I want to have as little negative impact on the climate and nature as possible. I want to have a very positive impact on my surroundings.

Once you get out there, you will be hooked. Whether the space you have to garden is large or small, you can make a difference to the world around you.

If you decide to grow your own food, you will feel so good, I promise you. In fact, let me know how you get on with your gardening journey. I really would like to hear what you have learnt and taken away from reading this book and ultimately what you have achieved because of it. And, if you would be so kind as to leave me a review, that would be most appreciated.

Social media contact @carolethegardenangel

Website www.thegardenangel.co.uk

Facebook: The Garden Angel

Acknowledgements

Writing a book is not easy! So, without the encouragement and a gentle push from a host of friends and family, this book would still be in my head. I would like to say a huge thank you to those people.

Firstly, Seamus for believing that I can write something that people would want to read and being so positive about it. My good friend Debs who has kindly read and given fantastic feedback on the draft versions of the book – you are an absolute star in more ways than one. Gemma, who first said to me that I could do this and then very patiently showed me how to use my laptop! And then gave me invaluable pointers to help me start writing. Family and friends who have been kind enough not to laugh in my face when I said that I was writing a book. Esme, who has been mostly snoozing by my side throughout this writing experience, and on waking encouraged me to take a break and spend some time walking around our garden together. My late parents, Archie and Helma, who instilled in me a thirst for knowledge and introduced me to the world of books. I am just sorry that neither of them saw this book published. Andrew, it's now your turn! And last but not least, a very big thank you to you for buying this book and reading it.

When you are sitting at your desk in the study of your house typing away, it is difficult to imagine that someone will eventually buy your book and read it. It's actually a very daunting thought, which I have parked somewhere at the back of my mind. But you did! So, I thank you all.

References

https://www.bethchatto.co.uk/

https://www.rhs.org.uk/soil-composts-mulches/soil-types

https://www.brainyquote.com/quotes/ mary_tyler_moore_130341

https://www.thespruce.com/how-to-test-soil-acidity- alkalinity-without-a-test-kit-1388584

https://www.rhs.org.uk/biodiversity/ ground-beetles-and-rove-beetles

https://www.rhs.org.uk/plants/trials-awards/ award-of-garden-merit/rhs-hardiness-rating

https://www.rhs.org.uk/propagation/softwood-cuttings

https://www.rhs.org.uk/propagation/layering

https://www.ruralsprout.com/ propagate-hardwood-cuttings/

https://www.rhs.org.uk/plants/types/perennials/dividing

https://www.greeninreallife.com/
propagating-plants-by-division/

https://www.thegardencontinuum.com/blog/the-6-
environmental-and-health-benefits-of-growing-your-own-
food

https://www.rhs.org.uk/propagation/
seed-collecting-storing

https://www.thespruce.com/
what-is-a-hybrid-garden-plant-1403422

https://www.permaculture.org.uk/design-methods/zoning

https://www.rhs.org.uk/advice/beginners-guide/
pruning-plants/pruning-shrubs

https://www.almanac.com/content/
pruning-guide-trees-shrubs

https://www.bobvila.com/articles/plants-that-repel-bugs/

https://www.gardenersworld.com/
plants/10-companion-plants-to-grow/

https://www.thespruce.com/
plants-that-repel-insects-4142012

https://www.rhs.org.uk/advice/health-and-wellbeing/
articles/a-scientists-view

https://www.rhs.org.uk/vegetables/crop-rotation

BBC Gardeners' World Magazine. (2024, January 16). Crop rotation. https://www.gardenersworld.com/how-to/grow-plants/crop-rotation/